THE TRICYCLE

THE TRICYCLE

A MEMOIR

SARA HARKNESS BOVITZ

PEPEM
PRESS

This is a work of creative nonfiction. All of the events in this memoir are true
to the best of the author's ability to mine her memory. Some names and
identifying characteristics have been changed to protect the privacy of
individuals.

Print ISBN: 979-8-9900933-0-0
Ebook ISBN: 979-8-9900933-1-7

Cover design by Kelly Berggren

PEPEM
PRESS

For Culby and Charlie
I love you infinity times two

#2020

By the time I could breathe, the world was already on fire. Oh, it had been happening all the while, it's just that I hadn't really noticed. I'd been, let's say... abstracted. It was kind of like when we were kids and we'd have a contest to see who could stay at the bottom of the pool the longest. When you were down there, looking up through the water, you could see the blurred shapes of friends cheering you on, but you couldn't hear what they were shouting, or even really tell who was who. There was just the vague sense that someone very far away wanted you to triumph. You could see the sun shining, but its warmth didn't reach you down in the coldest layer where you held yourself, curled in a ball, fighting the urge to breathe, because if you did — if you opened your airway even just a tiny bit — the water would rush in. Then you would be overcome, forced to jettison yourself back to the surface before you were ready, coughing and sputtering and gasping for air. And then suddenly, you would find yourself back among the hard edges of the world. And maybe all those people hadn't actually been cheering *for* you. And maybe the sun wasn't quite as warm as you'd remembered, a cool breeze licking your damp skin, raising a trail of goosebumps. And maybe, on the very worst day, the world had even come apart at the seams while you were gone.

~

When the results of the 2016 election were announced, I was as shocked and appalled as any good Lib. Not because I had even the slightest inkling of the monster our 45th president would reveal himself to be, but because it was just so *embarrassing*. The thought of having to listen to this buffoon for the next four years filled me with indignation, irritation, vexation, yes, but not fear — after all he'd be surrounded by smart professional people making the actual decisions, right? In hindsight, fear clearly would have been the more appropriate reaction, but to be honest I had other things on my mind, and failed to see beyond the caricature. I blame the hair: I mean how could we take that seriously?

On election day 2016, my husband JJ was at the City of Hope in southern California. I don't remember who, but one of our rotating team of family and friends must have been there with him because I was not, and that was the rule — he had to have a caregiver by his side at all times while he was receiving the experimental treatment, the miracle that would save him from the cancer eating away at his brain. I know I was home that week with our eight and ten-year-old sons, Charlie and Culby, because I remember explaining the election to them at the kitchen table, "That's how our government works, guys. Your person doesn't always win, but we *always* have a peaceful transfer of power, no matter what — that's the foundation of our democracy." I didn't realize then, that this was the second lie I would tell my children.

We didn't get our miracle in the end — or I should say, not the one we were desperate for. JJ died in the early hours of January 11, 2017 and, shattered by the weight of it, I sank down to the bottom of a very deep, very dark, very cold pool, curled up in a ball, and held my breath. When 45 was inaugurated nine days later, I frankly could not have cared less. He was just another blurry shape shouting from far far away.

1

THE BLIZZARD

It snowed 15 inches the night JJ died. Which may or may not sound substantial I suppose, depending on what winter is like where you live. We live in Portland, Oregon where yes, we know all about rain and even ice — but snow is another story, one that's typically reserved for days playing on the mountain. We're not quite sure how to manage it down here at sea-level.

Our town had three snowplows and they did their very best, but the streets lay untouched for days. People were skiing and snowshoeing all over the neighborhood, sometimes pulled along by a dog or two. Wide-ranging snowball fights and astonishingly creative snow sculptures sprang up everywhere — one front yard became an ice maze, the walls doused with water and allowed to freeze so that rainbows appeared when the sun struck it just so; another was transformed into a fairy garden, complete with tiny footprints left in the snow. Cars sat buried in driveways, replaced by all manner of DIY sleds on even the steepest hills — all evidence of barriers gone, limits erased. JJ would've loved it.

A blanket of magic had fallen over us, comforting somehow in its wholeness, hushed and surreal, softening the sights and muffling the sounds of the days that followed. Creating an intimacy, a coziness — a pain in the ass certainly — but rare and precious nonetheless. We decided that it was JJ dropping the mic with a chuckle on his way out. Typical.

Our home was filled with family and friends that last night, as it had been for the twenty-six days since the oncologist snipped our last strand of hope. A moment that stands alone, flash-frozen: We are in her office at the University of Washington Medical Center in Seattle. The walls are a dark color in my memory, and I could feel them closing in on me. JJ sits to my left holding my hand, his thumb pinning mine to stop it from rubbing back and forth — a habit I find affectionate and he finds annoying. He's wearing his poker face, not a hint of emotion peeks out, but he is jiggling his leg and intermittently clenching his jaw. He has on his faded green sweater, the one that's unraveling a bit at the cuff from when Zoey was a puppy and anything dangling anywhere was fair game, with a grey t-shirt underneath, and his requisite jeans. He still has his charcoal grey peacoat on, and the scarf my mom wove for him is around his neck; he's often chilly these days. The New Doctor sits across from us, her face is gentle, her eyes kind. We've never met her before; she had replaced Dr. M while JJ was at the City of Hope, and this was just a check-in while he was home for Christmas.

But as I had approached the hospital entrance where he was waiting for me while I parked the car, I saw several people hovering over a body crumpled on the ground. And someone else hurrying over with a wheelchair. I couldn't see the person being tended to, I didn't need to. A jolt of adrenaline, and then I was sprinting full speed between an endless row of cars that just kept getting longer and longer — like that nightmare when you're running as fast as you can, desperate to reach your goal, but no matter how hard you push you can't get any closer. By the time I reached his side, he'd been positioned in the wheelchair and complained only of some mild embarrassment. He had no memory of collapsing after I'd driven off. The New Doctor had called it a "drop attack", to do with the pressure on his brain. A bad sign.

She is quiet, contained. She speaks slowly, "I think it's time to talk about *hospice*." She leans forward and looks us in the eye as she says this. I can tell that she really does care. I can tell because I have been in her chair countless times. I'm a doctor myself, a hospitalist, which means I take care of people when they're sick enough to be in the hospital. I know this conversation. I know the struggle to hold back tears when telling someone the very worst news. I know how empathy can suck the life right out of you some days, particularly before you've learned how to compartmentalize. I know what it takes for her to say those words to a 43 year-old-man with two young sons at home.

She is doing such a good job I think, from a great distance. The reality lingers there on the horizon. Gathering storm clouds that hold a most violent purging, restrained only by time. Only for a moment.

We drove the three hours home in stunned silence that day, my thumb pinned the whole way. The shift in our world palpable but not yet *true*.

Then we were home, and JJ needed to use the bathroom.

We take it for granted when our brain and body are

connected, when our limbs respond to directions we're not even conscious of, but when that information highway is disrupted and you require help even to relieve your bowels, the loss of dignity becomes its own special torture. He was leaning on the cool marble surrounding the bathroom sink, his pants around his ankles as I was cleaning him up, when he turned to me and with a clarity that had been absent for weeks asked,

"So, am I basically dying right now?"

Time froze. The words hung there like icicles, then landed one by one. Precise. Cold and sharp, almost unnoticed until they started to melt, change shape, alter the balance of salt to water in my cells. Causing some to swell, others to shrink. Soon I'd be an emotional prune, shape changed so often and in so many directions that I'd be unrecognizable. But in that long cold moment, my husband was searching my face for the answer that he knew to be true, but could not quite believe.

"Yes, my love."

I wrapped my arms around him and the enormity of it oozed over us as we clung to each other. Seeping into every crevice and leeching all the colors from the world. We held each other close, leaning on that bathroom sink, for a thousand years.

∽

A few days later, I perched on the arm of the sofa pulled up beside the hospital bed in front of the bay window, the Christmas tree twinkling in the corner, my pillow and blanket still warm at my feet.

"Babe," I said, "what do you want me to tell everyone about coming to visit? Is it too much?" Even though his words had quickly abandoned him, sneaking out like guilty lovers in the night, we had developed a rhythm of communicating. He would use whatever tools he could muster to express a thought/request/idea, and I would summarize my interpretation. If I had missed the point he would shake his head and try again. Most of the time I was at least close, and he would signal our success by holding his hand palm up, long elegant fingers extended and bent toward his palm to meet his thumb, touching at the tips. Pursing his lips he would release a puff of air, "Pooohh" and open his hand, spreading his fingers wide, "like fireworks" he had said months before.

He shook his head in answer to my question, so I clarified, "Do you want me to put any limits on visits?" Head shake. "Do you want me to check with you first and see how you feel?" Vigorous head shake. "Do you want me to just tell everyone our door's open?"

"Pooohh!!"

Fireworks.

And so we were carried through those last weeks, wrapped up in a cocoon carefully crafted by our loved ones. Those who lived nearby were a constant presence. A forcefield surrounding us and absorbing all the details. Groceries? In the fridge. Laundry? Folded and in the hamper. Dinner? On the porch every night at six. Always ready to answer a frantic call.

One night, JJ fell and got wedged in between the sofa and the coffee table. I was in the kitchen and rushed in when I heard him cry out, but I just couldn't get him up off the floor and he was too weak to move himself. Humiliating. It was nearly midnight. I covered him with a blanket and sank down beside him with his head on my lap, while we waited for our friend Lee to come and help me get him into bed (luckily for us, Lee and his wife Jen lived just three blocks away with their twin girls). All he said when he answered the phone was, "I'll be right there."

Lee let himself in when he arrived, stomping the snow off of his boots, and shaking the crust of ice from the hem of his pajama pants. I put a pillow under JJ's head and moved around to face him, squatting down and pulling his arms while Lee got behind him and pushed his torso until he was sitting upright, his weight supported by Lee's chest. Then I bent his legs, so that his feet were planted on the floor, and we each put one of JJ's arms over our shoulders. It took several clumsy attempts, but we finally managed to deadlift JJ onto his feet, and the three of us stood there for a moment in an awkward embrace, catching our breath. JJ wore a veil of resignation. Lee wore one of concern. I don't know if my face reflected the torrent inside me in that moment, or if it was like a waterfall — the outline of each individual drop blurred by the enormity of the whole.

It was lucky for us too, that Lee's love language is food. He appeared again the next morning with a cast iron skillet in one hand and a bag of groceries in the other, "Thought you could use some breakfast," he said simply.

Later that day, we got the hospital bed, which delighted our nine and eleven-year-old sons who promptly requested electronic controls for their own beds. It arrived in a flurry, surrounded by its entourage of hand-held urinals and pink plastic bedpans with a bedside commode to complete the set, an adjustable table shaped like a sideways U, a shower chair that folded in half when not in use, a walker with a seat, which was helpful, and a wheelchair that we never used. There were boxes of latex gloves and stacks of adult diapers and packages of wet wipes. Bundles of individually wrapped mouth swabs and tubs of barrier cream and magnets for the fridge with the Hospice number on them, in extra-large print. And there were many, many medications.

JJ stayed in our bedroom while I rearranged the living room furniture and tried to tuck the evidence of our fate into corners and under tables, so that his view would be of joyful things, not just relentless reminders. But I saw his eyes rove around the room as he maneuvered his way from our bedroom to his new lair, as he paused for a rest on the seat of the walker, midway. I saw his face when he recognized the significance of it all. He took a deep breath. Then with great effort, he stood, and slowly finished the final leg of his trek.

That hospital bed proved invaluable toward the end, but it also tortured us for weeks after JJ died. It held sway by the front door, mattress deflated and metal frame folded up so it looked hollow, like a body without its soul. It stood there rudely, indifferent to our suffering. Our friend Brian pleaded with Hospice to either collect it or let him bring it to them — of course he understood that the roads were a mess, and of course the priority was getting equipment to people who were still alive and thus in need of it, but really it was unbearable, couldn't he just bring it to their warehouse himself? Someone finally put it outside, so at least we could avoid its stare.

Friends and family who lived farther away ebbed and flowed in a slow moving stream during those last weeks. Some stayed for a while, others flew in for a meal and then home again. We sat on chairs surrounding JJ, in front of the fire that was always lit, music playing in the background or a football game on the enormous TV I'd had installed in the living room as a surprise — I had vetoed a screen in the living room for years, but it was the last gift I gave him, and the only surprise I'd actually managed to pull off in our twenty years together. He only enjoyed it for a few weeks, but it's still there, and now when the boys and I snuggle up to watch *Star Wars* or *The Princess Bride* it's an odd comfort.

~

Our two sons sat perched on the edge of our bed, bewildered and forlorn, the night JJ died. "So who's going to take care of us now?" Culby asked urgently, "Are we gonna get a step-dad or what?"

A step-dad? JJ's still in the living room! I choked out a laugh that caught midway and morphed into a sob, eliciting quick looks of concern from both of them. The love of my life was lying down there, lifeless. It would be some time before two charming and remarkably capable 20-somethings would arrive in their ankle boots and eyeliner, and maneuver an unwieldy hearse through a foot of freshly fallen snow in the early morning darkness with the skill of seasoned race car drivers.

I hadn't known what to do when that final moment actually arrived. When I lay across his chest as he drew his last breath. When my heart cracked and my life force seeped out, grasping at the last tendrils of his as it drifted towards whatever comes next. It was just darkness. Beyond the breadth of my imagination. A black hole. I had been so focused on the last stage of his life. I hadn't even considered the first stage of his death.

2

MAGIC

(CIRCA 1995)

When I lived in Guatemala, during the last few years of their brutal civil war, I had a theory that magic happened there — that everything was so extreme, it left room for miracles to sprout in the wide open spaces yawning between the horrors and the heroes.

I was in my 20's, part of a small group doing development work in the remote villages strung across the mountaintops of the highlands. We were an informal operation working with Indigenous communities when they requested help with a water project or a school or a vaccination program, and whenever we started a project in a new area I would meet with the local Women's Group. My first question was always, "What would you do, if you could, to make your life better?" Their answers ranged from acquiring seed money to start a chicken co-op, to building a road to connect their pueblo to the market, to learning how to knit, because "It gets cold at night, and sweaters are too expensive to buy, but yarn is cheap — if we knew how to make them ourselves, that would help us."

So I started spending every other Tuesday afternoon perched on a steep hillside with a small group of women, feet propped on a rock to keep from sliding down the mountain, always with one eye out for venomous caterpillars. We chatted as we wound long skeins of brightly colored yarn into balls, and Alicia teased me about my abysmal tortilla making skills, "They're always so skinny on one side and so fat on the other," she giggled, "but the dogs like them."

And as I showed them how to cast-on, how to knit and to purl, they shared their stories.

Several years earlier the village had been attacked by the military, who claimed that the community was aiding the guerrilla fighters in their rebellion. The soldiers had come in the dark of night. They had robbed and beaten and raped. They had killed the animals and burned the crops. Then they had taken all the men and boys away. It wasn't until many years later that the mass grave was unearthed.

It just so happened however, that a young boy named Julio had been away that day. No one remembered why, but all agreed it was a great blessing. He was nineteen now, and the only man in the village — they relied on him. They were worried though, because there was something wrong with his heart.

"I can't believe what I just saw!" I shouted across the room to Dr. K as I burst through the operating room doors, tearing off the surgical mask and practically levitating in my excitement. "They literally stopped her tiny heart and it deflated like a bag, then they cut off a little piece of tissue from something else nearby, and patched the hole like it was a sock! And then they started her heart up again and it filled up like a balloon and now she's all pink and happy!"

Dr. K was a pediatric cardiologist who was part of a medical team that had come to Guatemala City to perform heart surgery on 30 infants and children. She looked at me and smiled, "So Sara, when is it, exactly, that you're going to medical school?"

I burst out laughing, "That's hilarious! No, I'm not a science person."

I had never even taken a biology class. My degree was in photojournalism, my science requirement had been Cultural Anthropology. I was just there to help coordinate, an extra set of hands to run errands or translate for the team as most of them didn't speak Spanish. Over the years I had gotten to know the staff at The Hospital, and Dr. B, who was the head of pediatrics. I was always hitting them up to help me with a Tuberculosis screening program or a family planning class up in the mountains, so I was happy to lend a hand — plus, it was fascinating.

I had watched as Dr. K evaluated the countless children brought by their families from all over Central America, small and blue and fragile. They stretched in an impossibly long line around the enormous hospital, a ribbon of brightly colored huipiles against the grey cement walls. Waiting with implacable patience for the slim chance to be one of the lucky ones. It spoke to me of hope, and of despair.

I was in awe of the mysteries Dr. K revealed just by looking at the color of the children's lips and listening to the rhythm of their blood; mesmerized by the images that appeared on a screen when she injected dye into the tiny vessels, outlining a beating heart no bigger than a walnut, pointing out where the hole or broken valve or misplaced vessel was, and describing what would be required to correct it.

It was miraculous, this gift the medical team brought. It was also a terrible burden for them to bear — forced to decide who would live and who would die. To know that for every family rejoicing there were ten who grieved. To accept that they were obliged to focus on those who had the best chance of survival, "The greatest good for the greatest number." Which meant dooming so many others they could have saved, if only there were more hours in a day. There were many sleepless nights.

So I was hesitant to make a request on behalf of Julio. I knew that the team had already stretched their capacity and added several more operations during what was supposed to be their "free-time". I also knew that Julio was nineteen years old, technically not even a pediatric patient. And, I knew that I did *not* know what was actually wrong with him, just that he needed some kind of heart surgery. But when I shared his story with the team, they responded with generosity and grace.

"Well the problem is, he needs a new valve and we don't have one," said Dr. K, explaining the results of the workup Julio had promptly undergone.

"But if you can find a valve, we'll put it in!" The surgeon was half-joking, but he had my complete attention. We would find a valve, magic happened here.

We found a valve — in fact the company that produced them sent a representative down to deliver it in person, and he wept when I introduced him to Julio's mother, Maria. She took his soft pale hands in hers, weathered and brown, patting them gently, and they shared a silent moment that required no words. No similar language or culture or history was necessary, they simply recognized each other's humanity.

The last weekend the team was in Guatemala, they piled into the back of our ancient black pickup with the rusted out floorboard, and we drove through the ubiquitous dust of the dry season, up the winding mountain road that led to Julio's village. It was perched on a hillside so steep that it was necessary to rope yourself to a tree and rappel down the mountainside in order to tend the crops, which grew at a startling angle, and was accessible only by foot for the last mile or so. As the nurses and doctors climbed out of the pickup, wiping the grit from their eyes, a group of women emerged from the surrounding forest, a burst of color against the muted greens and browns of the landscape. They had been waiting for us, tucked under the shade of the trees, bearing gifts for the team that had saved their only surviving son. They had even killed a chicken for lunch.

The afternoon was joyous. A celebration of life and of the things that bind us together as human beings. Of the things that matter.

～

It took another year or so for the seed that Dr. K had planted to germinate. When it struck me, I was on the back of a motorcycle bumping up a mountain trail. We were meant to be on our way with a medical team for a Tuberculosis screening and vaccination clinic, but instead, we were going to tell the village that it was cancelled because of a mix-up with the doctor's schedule.

If I were a doctor, I could just do it myself...

3

THE YEAR OF FIRSTS

I hadn't put any thought into which funeral home we would use. It simply didn't occur to me. Who did one call when their husband died at 3:30 in the morning in the middle of a blizzard? So I did the obvious thing, and Googled "Mortuary Near Me".

"I'm going to take care of you sweetheart," I said to Culby, who was still staring at me, wide-eyed and shell-shocked. I struggled to sound calm and pretend like I knew what that meant, "We lost your dad, but you still have a mom, and a brother, and we're going to figure it out together."

"But you go to work and we don't even see you for days sometimes," Culby said, agony leaking from his eyes, blazing a trail through the layer of grime that coated his face. *Good lord, when's the last time they bathed?*

"So who's gonna take us to school and make us food and stuff?" Charlie asked, trying to put some order to the world as it disintegrated around us.

"I promise, I'm not going back to work until we are all okay," *How can we ever be okay? What could that possibly look like?* "And when I do go back I'll find a way to make it work for all of us, as a family."

Culby's voice dropped to a whisper then, "But we're not a family any more, we're only three now instead of four."

That broke me. I squeezed out something pat, like, "We'll always be a family, my love, we're just a triangle now instead of a square — we're a tricycle," and we dissolved in a flood of tears. I have no idea how long we lay there. Time has a way of contorting itself around grief. But eventually our breathing calmed, and the tears slowed.

Finally, Charlie lifted his head up. "Well," he asked with a deep, shuddering breath, "can we at least have gummy bears for breakfast?"

∼

My sons were deeply skeptical of my ability to manage our life on my own, which was entirely appropriate. For as long as they could remember, JJ was our nucleus. He was the one who prepared all the meals, took them to school, washed all the clothes ("Do you even know how to do that, Mom?"). He mowed the lawn, took out the garbage, and fixed what broke. He brought me coffee in bed every single morning. When he chose to be our at-home parent he dove in with unrestrained enthusiasm — volunteering at school, coaching soccer and basketball, teaching the boys how to swim and fish and kayak and ski. He was the kind of dad who seeded the lawn by inviting all the neighborhood kids over for an epic grass seed battle. Who built them igloos in winter and water-sport obstacle courses on hot summer days. Which didn't always turn out well, to be honest.

One steamy August day for example, when Culby was a toddler, I walked out to the back yard and found JJ up on the playhouse strapping a hose to the top of the slide. At the bottom he had positioned the inflatable baby pool and filled it with water, "Look Doll — a water slide!" he shouted with glee as he turned the hose on to a trickle. Culby came toddling out of the house and ran over to his dad squealing in excitement. "Okay buddy, wanna try it out?" Culby scampered up the ladder. JJ helped him get positioned at the top and then let him go with a flourish. I watched in horror as my beloved child flew down the slide, into the baby pool, across the baby pool, out of the baby pool, and shot across the lawn like he'd been ejected from a T-shirt cannon. Giggling all the while, like it was the most fun he'd had in his whole two years.

I had worked long hours as a hospitalist for all of their lives. I *did* disappear for days at a time. They rarely saw me when I was on a work stretch, and when I was off we squeezed in all the fun things. As far as they could tell, Mom was just another family member who Daddy took care of, they never saw me do anything useful.

And so suddenly I found myself in a role that I had never assumed, and as it turns out, I was utterly inept. As a physician, I made life and death decisions every day, but when faced with the concept of preparing 21 meals a week, with the reality that laundry must be done more than once a month, and with the fact that children will not actually clean their bodies without direct supervision, I was completely at a loss. I mean, I know how to help a person in diabetic ketoacidosis, or rhabdomyolysis or septic shock, but how do you keep two devastated young boys in orbit when their star dies?

～

JJ was very clear — he wanted to be cremated and for his
sons to decide what they want to do with the ashes when
they're ready. We had discussed all this in generalities of
course, "Doll, I'll be dead — I'm pretty sure I won't be too
worried about it."

But when the time actually comes, you can never be
prepared for the job of choosing a vessel for your loved one,
nor for the visit to the funeral parlor. That place of quiet
suffering, everything brass and oak and red velvet. The
smell of potpourri and furniture wax hitting you as you
push open the heavy glass door. Everyone speaking quietly,
moving slowly, so as not to startle a grief-stricken patron out
of their protective shell. Furtive glances at the other families
that huddle together, *What is their story? Are they like me?
Do they find it hard to stand upright because their insides
have been hollowed out?*

"This will be a hard year for you," the funeral director
said. He peered kindly at me over his reading glasses, "The
Year of Firsts." And apparently the first First would be
choosing an urn. It mattered. It had to be exactly the right
one. It had to be the one that JJ would choose, not like the
outfits I put together for him that he tolerated (except for
that black turtleneck sweater which he hated because it was
itchy — but it looked so *good* on him!). In my memory
someone was there with me that day, but I can't picture
who, so maybe it's just JJ I felt, because he was exceedingly
present as I wandered slowly around the collection. I could
hear his quips in my ear and tried not to giggle out loud
because, well, that's just not appropriate in a funeral parlor.

In the far corner a porcelain tulip shaped urn, decorated
with light purple sprigs of lavender, stood tall on its own
pedestal like a Matriarch surveying her clan. An
overwhelming number and variety of vessels surrounded

her, grouped by material and style on long narrow tables tracing the perimeter, on floating ledges screwed into the oak paneled walls, on individual stands and multi-tiered shelves scattered around the room and continuing on into the next. *Who knew there were so many options?* I stopped and gazed around. I could hear JJ tease, "Oh no Doll, is this gonna be like picking out forks at William Sonoma? You'll be here all day!"

The light glinted off of a shiny silver cup on a small dais, resembling a trophy, "Well okay," I heard him say, "but only if you inscribe it with 'World's Greatest Dart Player' — the rest of the team'll argue, but they can't make too big a fuss cause they'd look like such assholes fighting with a dead guy." I stifled a chuckle. Some urns were simple and plain, others embellished and adorned. I thought about the correlation between a life and the vessel that was chosen to represent it, to hold it. *How many people would be pissed if they knew?* There was a golf themed one that sat on a bed of astroturf and had miniature golf clubs for handles, one dedicated to NASCAR complete with tiny wheels, and of course your choice of any college or professional sports team colors.

Then there it was, a beautiful wooden box, strong and solid but with gently rounded edges. *Just like you, Babe.* I picked it up. The finish was perfect. I ran my fingers over it, noticing how all the knots and swirls blended with the grain of the wood, adding character and interest and depth, and it reminded me of him. How he had this gift, this way of finding the beauty in imperfection. Of untangling a mess and gently extracting the threads, reweaving them into something new and revealing. "I could do that one, Doll," he whispered.

I held three small gold pendants in my hand, each one

with a fingerprint pressed into the metal — one mine, one Culby's, and one Charlie's. We put them in the box too, so he would never be alone.

~

The next day, my friend Meg quietly asked me if the boys had suits. "Suits?" I looked at her blankly.

"For the funeral?" she said softly.

"Wow," I said, fighting back a wave of nausea, "I hadn't even thought about that..."

"Don't give it another thought," she said, "I got it, just making sure they didn't already have something."

Three days later a box arrived from Nordstrom with two perfect little suits, with matching shirts and ties. I had, indeed, not given it another thought. I have thought of it many times since, though, marveled at the quiet generosity of my friend.

Then there was the question of what *I* would wear, which I hadn't thought about either — I mean, how do you dress for your husband's funeral? I stood for an eternity, there in front of our closet, the left side filled with an impressive collection of men's button down shirts and smelling faintly of his favorite cologne. A story lived with each breath. Memories so clear I could reach out and hold them if I just remembered hard enough... the salmon colored one with the subtle texture woven into the fabric, he'd found it at an open air market in a small town in northern Italy, and had taken great pride in his negotiating skills when he managed to get the price down by the equivalent of nearly $1 in just 45 minutes of haggling... the cream cotton one with the wide collar, embellished with blue and brown embroidery and finished with pearl snaps, that he often wore when we went out because he knew I loved it... the pale green linen one he wore to our rehearsal dinner the night before we married, when he had raised a glass to me and said, with a grin, "Doll, I promise never to say, *I love you, but...* and I promise always to say, *I love your butt*"...

I had to step away. This would require a new dress, one that would serve a singular purpose. I would make an effort, make him proud.

The neighborhood roads had yet to be plowed and were treacherous, but luckily there was a cute boutique just a few blocks from our house. I don't remember which of my girlfriends were with me, but I know they carried me through that day, that I couldn't have navigated it without them. We bundled up and ventured out, and were about halfway there when we ran into an acquaintance from work, "Hi Sara!" she called cheerfully, "This snow is crazy! How are you?"

My girls moved closer to me, one of them took my hand, "Well, my husband died the other day, so not great." I registered the horrified look on her face, and the awkward silence as she searched for some kind of response. I knew I'd just blindsided her, made her feel terrible, that I should say something, offer her grace, but I just couldn't bring myself to care.

The little shop was open despite the snow, warm and intimate. I felt safe there, buoyed by my friends as I tried on the outfits they brought to the tiny fitting room. I'm pretty sure I wept at some point, or maybe the whole time, or maybe not at all — the memory is covered in mist. I pulled on a simple black wool sweater dress, and caught my reflection in the mirror. *I am a hot mess,* I thought.

"Well, you are hot," JJ murmured in my ear.

~

For the service JJ's dad had one of our favorite photos of him (looking back over his left shoulder, blue eyes twinkling, and that contagious grin) blown up and mounted on foam board, with the words "You can't lose what's real" printed below.

I don't remember much of that day, but I do remember walking up the center aisle of the church with Culby and Charlie on either side of me in their new suits, and JJ in my arms, in that beautiful box. We set him down on a small table covered with a long white cloth, in front of the photo, and took our places in the pew. Three now, instead of four.

Afterwards, we gathered at Lee and Jen's, and the flashes of memory are random:

My friend Meredith's husband going out for more Bloody Mary mix:

"How many should I get?"

"I'd say three," Meredith said.

"OK, I'll get six," he replied.

"OK then, six," Meredith sighed, rolling her eyes.

"OK I'll get twelve," he said. She stopped talking to him at that point.

Shots of Slivovitz, a Slovenian plum brandy that goes down like a chemical fire, and is required at all meaningful events in the Bovitz family. JJ would explain here that the original spelling of Bovitz was Bevac, but as so often happened it was misspelled when his Great Grandfather arrived on Ellis Island from Slovenia. He felt a deep connection to his heritage, and when we visited the Slovenian capital Ljubljana a year after his first surgery, he had joyfully pointed out every passerby with a familiar aquiline nose, "Look Doll — that person has my nose! And that one!"

I remember the dining room table covered with a beautiful spread of food that Jen had arranged, and I'm sure was delicious, although I don't think I tasted it. And JJ's beloved childhood friend Susan, who looks remarkably like an angel when the sun hits her blonde curls just right, bringing the leftovers to a homeless camp afterward, exactly as he would have wanted.

Someone told me I was "doing a great job." I remember wondering what that meant.

There was a slide show playing on the TV, a million photos, a million memories. I couldn't watch for too long.

I remember tears in eyes that I'd never seen cry, and laughter shared by strangers newly bonded.

But mostly, I remember feeling like my skin was on inside-out.

～

Before I went to bed that night, I turned off the fire that had been lit since we came home from that final appointment with the oncologist. Since the beginning of the end.

Goodnight my love.

4

THE GUARDIAN

(1996)

My parents sent a limousine to pick me up at the airport when I arrived back home in Chicago from Guatemala in the summer of 1996, not because we're fancy, but because I had too much stuff to fit into their Acura. Also, I suspect they held some trepidation regarding my ninety pound Guatemalan-German Shepherd Kan (pronounced *Kaan* — short for Kukulkan, the Feathered Serpent God) and their leather seats, although they would probably deny that. The limo was long and black, with tinted windows and a stocked bar, and the driver wore a chauffeur's cap. Kan and I sat in the far back. Cardboard boxes, carefully packed with the treasures I'd collected over the years, filled the vast expanse between us and the driver, requiring use of the intercom for communication. I rolled the window down so that Kan could stick his head out, chomping at the wind, and he rode like that the whole way, delighting passersby who honked and waved.

"So what did you miss most of all while you were

gone?" the driver asked over the intercom as we neared my neighborhood in Evanston.

"Hot baths, sushi, and lattes," I said without hesitation. Ironically, although some of the best coffee in the world is grown in Guatemala, at that time it was all exported, and a good cup was hard to come by.

"Well," he grinned at me in the review mirror, "we can take care of one of those right now — let's give them something to talk about." He slowed down and double parked right in front of the busy Starbucks on Central Street, a quaint strip of neighborhood shops near my childhood home. It was not subtle.

"Oh! Okay, great — thanks!" I moved to open the door and hop out, hoping to be quick because we were blocking traffic and people were starting to pretend not to stare, but he was already standing outside the open window, speaking to me past Kan's head, loudly and with great formality.

"And what can I get for you Ma'am?" he asked with a wink. "A latte, perhaps?"

Beyond him shoppers and coffee drinkers paused, whispering to each other, speculating on who could be in that stretch limo with the German Shepherd keeping watch — it was obviously a Very Important Person. I smiled a thank you and leaned back, out of view, struggling to wrap my head around the immeasurable gap between where I'd started the day, and where I presently found myself. The leap from poverty and war and despair, to privilege and frivolity and shopping. It made my head spin.

The latte was delicious, though.

∼

It started in the cereal aisle. With its rows and rows of options, so many that by the time you reached the end you'd forgotten the beginning. I'd become accustomed to two or three dusty boxes to choose from at the tienda, and was too overwhelmed to start over, so I grabbed the one in front of me and scurried over to the toilet paper aisle, which proved to be a mistake.

In Guatemala there had been one kind of toilet paper — the kind that was available. It was all recycled, and came in the pink or tan variety, and you bought what the tienda had. It was the toilet paper aisle that did me in. The sheer obscenity of it. I stood there, gazing at a snow white wall that stretched as far as I could see. A countless variety. Each package proclaiming the highest absorbency or the softest feel or the most sheets per roll. I turned around, and the wall encircled me. I was in a crevasse of toilet paper. About to be crushed by an avalanche of triple-ply-aloe-infused sheets. My heart was pounding, and I needed to move. To escape. To breathe. It was just too much. I abandoned my shopping cart, and ran for the door.

Later, I called Dana. We had found each other in Guatemala, our friendship immediate, deep, and lifelong. Together, we had carried bags of cement to the tops of mountains and distributed the toothbrushes we had cajoled Colgate into donating. We had swum in underground lakes and slept in deserted ruins after whispered conversations around candle lit ball courts. We had borne witness to unfathomable cruelty and miraculous courage. We had shared a singular time. She would get it.

Dana had left Guatemala for Portland, Oregon, where she was currently working for a quirky porcelain artist who just happened to be looking for an office manager. "It's a much easier re-entry in Portland," she said. "I promise."

≈

If I was actually going to go to medical school, I had a long road ahead. It would require two years of the basic science classes I had so assiduously avoided throughout my educational career, before I could even sit the entrance exam. Then a year of applying. Then four years of school, and a minimum of three years as a Resident.

"Mom, do you realize I'll be almost *forty* by the time I'm done?" I said, with the incredulity of the not yet thirty-something.

"Well sweetheart," she looked at me and smiled, "I hate to tell you this, but you're going to be forty anyway. What you need to ask yourself, is what you want to be doing."

She's pretty smart, my mom.

≈

Kan and I drove the 2,000 miles from Chicago to Portland in a stranger's car. Not with the stranger, but rather for him, like a courier of sorts. It was a nondescript four door sedan, beige, I think, and boxy. And I remember it had thick shag carpeting, which struck me as an interesting choice.

We drove the whole way with the windows down and the Gipsy Kings blasting from my little yellow boombox, Kan stretched out on the front bench seat, his head on my lap. It reminded me of driving the dusty roads of Guatemala, in the old black pickup with the rusted out floorboard. Kan had gone everywhere with me there — everywhere that is, except the bank, because he made the armed guards nervous and they wouldn't allow him inside. It was fascinating really, the effect he had on grown men with a penchant for machismo, even those armed with automatic weapons.

There weren't many German Shepherds in Guatemala then, or many dogs of his size at all really, and people frequently asked me if he was a wolf — usually from a safe distance and with an apprehensive look in their eye. He was given to me when he was twelve weeks old by a British couple who had bought him from a breeder, only to learn days later that they had to return to England, where strict rabies precautions meant that the three-month-old puppy would have had to spend his next six months in quarantine. I'd never had a dog before, never had a pet at all in fact, unless you count my family of Sea Monkeys or Homer, my Pet Rock, but I had recently been thinking about adopting one of the many street animals a friend regularly rescued and found homes for. I had met a few dogs and they were all very sweet but, none of them had been *my* dog — it's kind of like a first date I suppose, either there's a spark or there's not.

Then I met Kan. And it was like one of those old Hallmark commercials, with a reunited couple running across the beach toward each other in slow-motion, arms outstretched, as the sun sets over the ocean. He bounded straight to me, his enormous head and paws comically out of proportion to his little three-month-old body, and leapt into my arms. It was love at first sight.

Kan morphed from a goofy puppy into a full-grown dog with adult responsibilities in a heartbeat. He quickly assumed the role of my guardian, a shift I noticed for the first time when I took him to the beach one weekend. We were walking along the shore near sunset, and up ahead, standing at the very edge of the waterline, was a man wearing a broad rimmed straw hat and holding a fishing rod.

He deftly cast the line, waited a beat, and slowly reeled it back in. Then he did it again. And again. His motions were practiced, rhythmic, soothing. A meditation.

Suddenly — Kan came running from out of nowhere and charged by, spraying me with sand as he passed. He stopped abruptly several yards ahead, and stood stock-still and silent, staring intently at the man calmly casting his line. As I drew closer, Kan turned and began to nudge me, pushing me away from the shore and guiding me in a semi-circle away from the water and in an arc around the man, keeping himself in-between me and the stranger at all times. At first I didn't realize what he was doing, and tried to continue walking along the water's edge, but Kan was simply not having it. He moved directly in front of me and let out a short high-pitched bark, reprimanding me for not paying attention to his instructions. My toes didn't touch the water again until we were well past the fishing man, who watched the scene with a nervous smile, but never stopped casting his line, and reeling it back in.

A few months later we were driving the dusty road down from the mountains, Kan lying stretched out with his head on my lap as we bumped along, when a man in a military uniform stepped out of the trees and into the middle of the dirt road. He raised his left hand, cocked his wrist, and ordered me to stop. I did as he said, mostly because of the machine gun in his other hand, and the ammunition belt slung across his shoulder.

"Give me a ride into town," he called from his position about ten yards ahead of me, and my stomach lurched. There had been a series of attacks on women by soldiers recently, women who were forced off the road and raped in the brush.

"I'm happy to give you a ride, but you'll have to go in the back," I said, pointing to the bed of the truck.

"No," he said, walking toward the passenger side of the pickup, both hands on the gun now, "I'll ride in front, with you."

My heart was going so fast I was sure I would use up all my beats, and as the soldier reached for the door handle, I said "I don't think you want to do that." I took my hand off of Kan's head, and he popped up, spinning around with his back up and his teeth bared, emitting a low pitched growl that sent shivers rippling down my spine. The soldier leaned down to look in the window, and Kan erupted, barking with a ferocity that caused the soldier to jump back in alarm, and trip over his own feet. He stumbled and fell backwards, landing on his backside with a thud. I was about to throw the truck into drive and speed away, but he was gripping the machine gun with a look of such fury that it gave me pause, *Is this truck faster than a bullet?* There are few things as dangerous as a wounded ego with a weapon.

Kan was still barking, and trying to squeeze himself out of the half-open window, while the soldier scrambled back to his feet and glared at us, his face a mixture of wrath and fear. I was petrified. I waited for him to raise the gun and shoot Kan or me or more likely, both of us. But then he looked at me, and said flatly, "I'll ride in the back." Kan sat backwards, keeping watch on the soldier, all the way to town.

I chuckled to myself at the memory, and scratched Kan's ears as I sang along to *Volare* with all of my breath, a ridiculous smile plastered across my face. I was bubbling with excitement, anticipation, curiosity. It felt exactly right, driving across the plains and over the mountains, into our new chapter. My guardian by my side.

As we pulled off the highway and started across the Morrison Bridge, I saw Portland for the very first time, and my heart skipped a beat. The sky above was a deep cerulean blue, not a cloud to be found, and the light was crisp, so clear as to feel surreal. On either side of us, ten other bridges stretched across the Willamette River, connecting East to West; each one distinct, from the northernmost St. Johns Bridge with its Gothic arches and oxidized copper hue, to the most southern Sellwood Bridge, a simple steel truss affair. On the far side of the river lay downtown, and beyond rose the West Hills, draped in green. It felt magical. Like a gift waiting to be unwrapped.

I took a left on Broadway, and slowed to let a bald man with a long grey beard braided into three plaits who was wearing a peasant skirt with rainbow striped knee socks but no shoes, carrying a cat, and riding a unicycle, pass. At the corner, a vigorously mustachioed man with a neon green mohawk and vivid tattoos in lieu of a shirt, held hands with a woman carrying a briefcase and dressed in a conservative navy business suit with sensible heels, while they waited for the light to change. I was distracted for a moment, as I passed a car with a mannequin's severed foot sporting a bright pink pump attached to the roof like a unicorn's horn, surrounded by a field of troll dolls of every imaginable iteration, and had to hit the brakes to avoid yet another unicycler — this one dressed in a kilt and playing the bagpipes. I still can't figure out how he did that through the Darth Vader helmet that completed his outfit. It also begged the question, is it easier to ride a unicycle in a skirt?

Dana was meeting us after work, so in the meantime, Kan and I wandered over to a nearby cafe. I spotted a free table outside, and as we were walking over to it, the cafe door opened and a young man in a large electric wheelchair came rolling out. (A side note here — one of the things I learned in Guatemala was to always lift your feet up when riding a motorcycle near a dog. Because when a person is on a motorcycle, a dog doesn't see a person plus an object, it just sees one big, loud, scary creature. It freaks them out. More than once, I'd had to shake an angry dog off of my Doc Martins). So when Kan saw this mysterious half-human-half-machine coming toward us, he immediately sprang to my defense, jumping in front of me, growling and barking like mad. Everyone around us froze, except the young man, who smiled, and said calmly, "He needs to switch to decaf."

We both burst out laughing, and a friendship was born.

His name was Paul, and he first shared his story with me that afternoon over lattes, Kan's head resting on his knee. When he was 17 and a senior in high school, he'd been visiting his older brother at college in California, the same college he was planing to attend the following year. They'd spent the day at the beach, diving over waves and generally horsing around.

"A wave came, and I dove over it," he spoke softly but clearly, "but there was only an inch of water on the back side. I dove straight into the sand. And I knew instantly," he grimaced slightly, "I knew I broke my neck. I knew I was paralyzed, I was face down in the sand, and I couldn't turn myself over. I would've drowned if my brother hadn't been right there to pull me out."

"I just can't imagine what went through your head in that moment," I said. Literally, unable to imagine it.

"*I hope he doesn't get here in time,*" he said, with a wry smile. "That was the first thought that went through my mind. *Just let me die.*"

"So... How do you feel about that now?" I asked, after a long moment.

"Now? Now, I'm grateful."

~

I fell asleep snuggled up with Kan on Dana's sofa that night, reflecting on two truths, oblivious to their prescience:

1) The Fates are capricious and unsentimental.

2) It is possible to survive The Very Worst Thing.

5

FIRST VALENTINE'S DAY

Valentine's Day was never our favorite, mostly because it's predictable, lacks the element of surprise. I suppose for those of us who are not gifted romantics (myself, for example) it serves as a helpful reminder, but I was lucky enough to marry a man who delighted in weaving a little romance into every day. He never needed a reason to bring home flowers, or leave a love note on my pillow. And he adored a grand gesture. For JJ, half the fun was the planning of it, and he would then go to extreme lengths to execute said plan.

So it was that one warm spring evening, not long after we were married, I had arrived at our new house in Spokane ahead of schedule, in hopes of surprising him. "I should be there tonight by ten," is how we had left it that afternoon, but it was well before then when I pulled in to the left side of the two car garage, beige with white trim to match the house on the corner lot with the big maple tree in front; the sun was down but it was still warm and the sky was sparkling.

I heard music playing and when I opened the door into the back yard it was aglow, lit up like a beautiful Diwali festival. There were candles everywhere — lining the walkway, hanging from tree limbs, tucked into nooks I hadn't even known were there. A shadow garden flitted over the white fence that was too tall for current codes but had been grandfathered in, we were grateful for the privacy. As I walked toward the house I spotted him, up on the main part of the deck. Lying on a blanket. Two glasses of wine and a strategically placed plate of cheese and fruit in front of him.

Completely. Adorably. Naked.

"Welcome home Doll," his grin was mischievous, "I was thinking, we've blessed all the rooms of our first house, but we haven't christened the deck yet..."

"Babe, we haven't talked since this afternoon, how did you know when I'd be home? How long have you been lying there?"

"Looks like exactly the right amount of time," he said, handing me a glass of wine.

But you can't leapfrog over February 14th, even if it never was your favorite, and Valentine's Day that first year without him was long and lonely. I remembered at the last minute that of course the boys were in elementary school and therefore needed valentines for their classmates, so I went scurrying to the store for a couple boxes of those pre-printed cards, with a packet of semi-crushed sweethearts attached. *At least it's not pencils,* I thought, as I grabbed some stuffed animals and candy for Culby and Charlie.

JJ's parents sent me flowers, which was so incredibly

thoughtful, but also resulted in an extremely awkward moment when I opened the door to the delivery guy and promptly burst into tears. And believe me when I tell you, it was neither dainty nor poetic. There was no misty gaze off into the distance, with a lone tear spilling down my cheek... No. It was ugly crying, the kind that contorts your face and produces gallons of snot. The kind that seizes your diaphragm, and your ability to speak. The kind that leaves you swollen and exhausted. The poor delivery guy stood there speechless, mouth slightly agape, holding a dozen red roses and not sure what to do with them, "Ummm... should I just set them down here?" he asked, taking a step back and eying me anxiously. I couldn't collect enough air to form words, so I just nodded, and he placed them gently on the stoop with a sympathetic look. As he turned to jog back to his van he called out reflexively "Have a great day!" which struck me as deeply hysterical. I stood there in my front doorway, for how long I could not say, laughing and sobbing with equal abandon. So awash in raw emotion that I wondered if I might just melt away. *Will it always be like this?*

I faked my way through that afternoon as the boys proudly displayed their shoeboxes decorated with paper hearts and doilies, oohing and ahhing over all of the elaborate handmade cards with homemade treats and personalized messages from their classmates, which I was pretty sure must have taken their respective adults a significant amount of time to produce. *That's a high bar,* I thought as I squirreled away an especially elaborate origami creation for future reference, *did JJ do that?* This at-home-parent thing was gonna take a while to get the hang of.

Immediately after JJ died people started mentioning The Center, an organization that provides support and resources for grieving children and families. People mentioned it again, and again, and again. But I was so overwhelmed and disorganized at that point that it was all I could do to make sure my children had pants on when we left the house, much less navigate another whole process that actually involved saying the words "Their father died."

"It's *your* fault Daddy died!" Culby gripped the bannister and glared at me through his tears from the top of the stairs "*You* made him go do the science experiment and now he won't ever take us fishing again!" The term "science experiment" had been an unfortunate choice when explaining the clinical trial JJ had been part of — I can only imagine what images that left seared onto his eleven-year-old mind. And it hadn't occurred to us to clarify that although I was *a* doctor, I wasn't *Daddy's* doctor.

Culby ran to his room sobbing, and I stood rooted there. I couldn't move. I couldn't think, or hear, or even feel anything. It was like being encased in a fluffy down pillow, everything muffled and far away, only if instead of down it was filled with those tiny burrs that stick to your shoes at the beach. And then I was being suffocated, I couldn't breath. I released the bottom end of the banister which I hadn't realized I was squeezing so hard, and turned to walk into my bedroom. I slowly closed the door, and sat on the end of the king size bed that filled most of the room, ("I mean what else do we do in the bedroom, Doll?" he'd said with a wink).

I can't do this by myself.

The next day I called The Center, and we were placed in a group with other children and their grown-ups, all at various points in the grieving process. When we arrived at the big craftsman house that had been meticulously adapted to serve its current purpose we were given sharpies and name tags, and we joined the circle of broken families. A few words of greeting, and then the children went off to have their own circle, where those who wanted to speak did, while others held their suffering closer. Culby hated that part, "I don't always want to sit there and hear everyone else's sad story. Sometimes I'm having a good day and I just want to have a good day." Charlie on the other hand found it comforting, "It makes me feel like we're not the only ones."

Afterwards they were free to explore and experience whatever spoke to them, always with a trained volunteer nearby, ready to help guide them through whatever rabbit hole they might tumble into. There were rooms for music, with guitars and horns and countless percussion instruments. A dress up room, with a stage complete with a sound system for impromptu performances. A room set up like a hospital, with a bed and an IV pole, white coats and a real stethoscope hanging on a hook. There was a game room with pinball and ping pong and arcade games, a volcano room with nothing but soft pillows where they could scream and cry and rage as much as they needed, and an art room stocked for all kinds of therapeutic projects. There was even a splatter-paint room where the walls were lined with paper, and the kids donned full-body smocks before flinging their pain with all their might, releasing their inner Jackson Pollocks. That was Charlie's favorite. Culby gravitated to the outdoor play area, with the basketball hoop.

Meanwhile, the adults were led up a wide curved staircase and into one of two rooms. Mine was large and open with windows at the far end looking out over the street, but I remember it as dim. An eclectic collection of about a dozen chairs was arranged around the room, I chose an ancient brown corduroy lounger that tilted back and to the left as I sat down, and I noticed that as people came in they seemed to go directly to a specific spot. *I hope I'm not in somebody's seat.* I was the only new member of the group, the others had been together for varying lengths of time, and greeted each other warmly as they came in. It felt a bit like joining a new lunch table in a middle school cafeteria.

The conversation started with a round of introductions to include your name, what your loss was, and your relationship to the child or children you were there to support.

"I'm Liz. My husband died of colon cancer four years ago, and I'm here with my son who is twelve."

"My name's Bob and my ex-wife died in a car crash eighteen months ago. My daughter Kim was with her at the time, she's nine now."

"Hi, my name is Carrie and I'm here with three of my four children, my oldest didn't want to come today. Their father died of brain cancer three-and-a-half years ago and we've been coming here ever since. But he's a teenager now and doesn't think he needs it anymore."

Every nerve in my body stood at attention. I looked at her with an intensity that probably bordered on rude, *three-and-a-half years*. She appeared normal, like a functional human being. She was pretty, her dark shoulder length hair pulled back in a low ponytail, her delicate features arranged in a neutral expression. She sat upright in her chair, ankles crossed, and her voice was soft but clear. Her eyes were not swollen and bloodshot. She did not tremble. Was she faking it? Wearing a facade to match her sweater set? Holding the pieces of herself together by will alone? If not... could that mean there was hope?

Others were speaking as we continued around the circle, but I was distracted, stealing glances at Carrie and wondering about her story, until suddenly it was my turn, "Hi my name is Sara." To my horror I started weeping as soon as I opened my mouth but I kept going anyway because everyone was looking at me and I just wanted it to be over, "My husband died of brain cancer, too, two months ago." I glanced up at Carrie and she gave me a gentle nod of encouragement. "And I'm here with my two sons who are nine and eleven." Someone kindly offered me a tissue.

I didn't talk after that, or even hear much of what was said over the next hour. I was focused entirely on holding it together, *I can do this I can do this I can do this.* But when the moderator asked if anyone had any questions or thoughts they'd like to share I heard myself ask "So how long does it take? I mean, to get to where you can even start? Because, it's not even real for me yet... I feel like I'm living in this weird parallel universe..."

A murmur rounded the group and looks of compassion and sympathy came from every direction. "Well," Carrie leaned forward with her elbows on her knees and clasped her hands, "for me, to be honest, it's only in the last couple of months that I've started to feel like I'm sort of waking up, so I'd say about three years?" A wave of knowing nods rippled around the room.

But.

That's not possible.

No.

I can't do this for three years.

Absolutely not.

Three years?

～

JJ loved that his birthday fell on St Patrick's Day. He often said it was the best day to be born because "everyone's always up for a party!" Every year I made corned beef and cabbage for him, although after he got a smoker he took over the corned beef part (best Christmas gift I ever gave him!). Everyone came over, we wore silly hats and sat around the table for hours after dinner, it was always a fun night. So it was obviously the night to have a Celebration of Life for JJ, a chance for all the people whose travel to the service in January had been upended by the series of winter storms, to gather and reminisce. We took over the top floor of our favorite bowling alley, where there was a large bar surrounded by cocktail tables, with a smaller room off to the side for food and a video game arcade for the kiddos on the other end.

Of course JJ had to be there, so we set him up at a table in the front, with a glass of Irish whiskey and a Guinness, and we put a book beside him for people to leave a thought or two. Friends and family came from all over, sharing moving toasts, hilarious memories, and embarrassing stories. There was much laughter, and quite a few tears. All the guys wore one of JJ's button down shirts, which caught me off guard a few times, but it was warm and comforting nonetheless, and very, very emotional. As the party was winding down and I was gathering up all the kids for a sleepover at our house, our friend Brian came up, "Sara, we want to take JJ to Sassy's — what do you think, would that be OK?"

"You mean Sassy's the strip club?!"

"Yep," he said with an impish grin.

"You mean literally take him? In his box?"

"Yes! You know he'd be up for it." It was true. And Brian would know, he and JJ had been like brothers, loving and arguing with equal ferocity. Childhood friends, they were partners in adventure — always off to climb Smith Rock or raft the John Day River or camp in the Rocky Mountains or surf on the Oregon coast. They were both big hearted and generous of spirit, and were never happier than when sharing the joy, and by joy, I mean shenanigans. Brian was at JJ's side in the park on the day we met, in the church on the day we were married, and in our living room on the day JJ died. He and Meg, his wife, slept on the floor in front of the fire that night, trapped at our house by the blizzard. Brian lay awake, just like I did, listening. And when JJ's last breath faded away, his heart broke too.

"Well, you're right," I laughed, wiping away a tear, "he would be up for it — but Brian I swear to God, if you lose him I will never forgive you."

So the guys, along with my little sister Devin and JJ's little sister Kate, walked up the street to the strip club — famous for also serving strip steak — and set JJ up on the rail with a PBR. Of course Devin had to snap a picture of him sitting there, but it turns out that taking photos is really frowned upon in strip clubs, and she was promptly expelled. Luckily the bouncer was kind and she charmed him into letting her stand in the doorway and duck her head inside to take furtive sips of her beer while she chatted up the random revelers passing by. So it was that the last photo of that night came to be the one with JJ's guys and our two little sisters, holding him aloft in that beautiful box under the neon pink Sassy's sign.

~

I took the boys to Palm Springs a week later for spring break, with two other families. We'd gone there the year before too, and had a wonderful time exploring Joshua Tree — JJ with at least one child on his shoulders at all times — and taking the kids to the obscenely wasteful water park in the middle of the desert, where he'd led the charge to the highest water slide. Back at the house, the dads and kids had romped in the pool while the moms sipped cold drinks and read trash mags. At night we slathered the kids faces with Aquafor to soothe their dry cheeks, or as they called it "crackly face" and took turns making dinner on the grill, with the Avett Brothers playing in the background.

This time we had also rented a lovely house with a pool, and we were looking forward to some sunshine and friendship. It wasn't until we actually arrived that the reality hit us — of course it was different, we were surrounded by echoes. We went back to Joshua Tree, but entered from a different point, no awe-inspiring rock formations to scramble up, just desert scrub brush and an occasional lizard or cactus in bloom. The water park was still there, rising like a mirage in the middle of the desert, but it wasn't as sparkly as I remembered and the boys weren't as interested in the high slide. At one point I glimpsed a man from behind who's shape and movements were so familiar it stopped me mid-stride. I knew it wasn't JJ of course, but I couldn't take my eyes off him until he turned around, and gave me an awkward smile that said, "You're staring at me, and it's weird."

We still took turns making dinner, but now it was my job where it had always been his. We still romped in the pool but now I assumed the role of adult romper, and I couldn't toss them nearly as far as JJ could. There was still "crackly face" to be soothed, games to be played, fun to be had, but it was as if a cosmic dimmer switch had been adjusted. Everything was dulled. Then came the windstorm, knocking out electricity and filling the pool with sand and debris. Covering everything with a fine layer of grit, so that even the simplest thing like sitting down on a patio chair was uncomfortable, even painful, until you cleared it away.

It felt appropriate.

There were flashes during that week when it felt almost normal, and for a second I could breathe. Moments when I could see the blue of the sky, and feel the warmth of the sun; could hear the kids laughing and even find a smile on my own face. But then I always remembered. I still reached for him every night, and I was still shocked when he wasn't there. I relived that moment of loss every single time.

When we got home from Palm Springs and walked in the front door, I was struck by how hollow the house felt, like a seashell after its animal has died or moved on. I was consumed by an intense hatred of the brown leather sofa where I'd slept beside JJ's hospital bed. I detested the sandy color of the walls, and couldn't stand to look at our favorite rug which we'd brought back with us from Spokane. All I could see was his absence. It was everywhere.

The next day I ordered a new sofa and rugs, and bought gallons of white paint. White, because we needed light, we needed air. We also needed inspiration, so I found a book of stunning photographs of natural wonders around the world and papered one of the dining room walls with them. My favorite is of an ant. She is standing upright on her back legs and pushing along a single drop of water. It towers over her, at least twice her height, and reflected in that perfect sphere is the whole world, only upside down.

When the boys asked me what I was doing, I told them I was making us a Wall of Awe — because sometimes we need a reminder that on the other side of grief lies hope. And that there is still a big beautiful world out there waiting to be explored. Some day. Once it rights itself again.

6

THE BACK LOT

(1960'S-1980'S)

My earliest memories are ephemeral — feelings, really, not so much defined moments or concrete images. I am not one of those people who can remember their second birthday, or the first time they tasted chocolate. What I remember is feeling safe, and loved. Cozy.

I was born in June of 1967, it was the *Summer of Love*, and the good vibes stretched from Haight-Ashbury to New York to London. The season was brief, however, and my parents divorced in short order. My mother and I moved from Boston to Chicago, to be near her brother who was a man of his time, both an activist and a hippie, and also a beloved teacher at a suburban high school. That is, until he was fired for declining to grade his students based on metrics which he argued were invalid. When he had been informed by the school administration that the assignation of grades was non-negotiable, he responded by asking his students to reflect on their own work over the term, on the degree of their effort and the depth their participation, and then to grade themselves appropriately. He, in turn, assigned their official grade based on how honestly they had judged themselves. The school board was not amused.

We lived close to him, in a quaint second floor apartment in Old Town, a neighborhood of young Bohemians awash in the romantic idealism of the day. By all accounts, it was a mosaic of colors and textures and scents and sounds, thrumming with life, teeming with passions. Hippies in peasant blouses and bell bottoms marched for civil rights and sat-in for reproductive freedom, protested against the Vietnam War and rallied for women's liberation. Pete Seeger played at the Old Town School of Folk Music, and John Belushi joined the Second City theater group. Everyone ate ribs at the Twin Anchors tavern.

On Saturdays, my mom would collect her waist length auburn hair into a ponytail at the nape of her neck and attach me to her bike in a manner that would probably earn her a visit from Child Protective Services these days, and we would ride east, to Lincoln Park. We would wander around the zoo, or build sand castles on the beach, or have a picnic in the shade of an old oak tree. We might stop for some groceries on the way home, and have a spontaneous dinner party around the big table fashioned from a reclaimed door which had been carried home from the aptly named Door Store down the street. Or we might pop over to my uncle's apartment for a visit, sitting out on the back landing while he smoked the cigarettes he rolled himself, and the occasional joint.

"It was a fun time," my mom says with a nostalgic smile, when I ask her about it.

I wonder sometimes, what path my mother's life might have taken if she had been simply a young divorcee then, as opposed to a young divorcee with a child on her hip. What choices she might have made, where they might have led her. Her responsibilities as a single mother kept her on the fringe, but she worked with the underground Abortion Counseling Service of Women's Liberation, known as The Jane Collective, nonetheless, and brushed shoulders with the occasional Black Panther. And then there was the whirlwind romance with a dashing young Irishman who was in Chicago to raise funds for the Irish Republican Army. He begged her to return to Ireland with him, and when I asked her why she didn't go she said, "Because I had a child! I couldn't bring you into the middle of a war zone!"

"So, if you hadn't had me, would you have gone?" I asked.

She paused thoughtfully for a moment, "Probably," she said, with a cheeky grin.

Then she met her person. He was smart and handsome and witty, and he was remarkably patient with me — up to a point. One day, I was being naughty in the way of the four-year-old, I'm not sure what I was up to, but I've never had a very retiring personality so I'm sure I'd done something exceptionally obnoxious. He was looking after me, as my mom wasn't around, and reprimanded me firmly for my misbehavior. I was outraged. Who did this *man* think he was? He wasn't my *mom*! I wheeled around to face him, hands on my hips, "You're not the boss of me!" I proclaimed, glaring at him with fury and stomping my foot for emphasis, "I *amn't* your kid!"

I didn't know how wrong I was — grammatically, or otherwise.

They were married the day after my fifth birthday, in front of the living room fireplace in our new house in the suburbs. I remember going with them to the artisan's workshop where they had created the molds for their wedding rings, pressing their fingers into warm wax in a random pattern — the result was two weighty gold bands, hers covered with his fingerprints, and his with hers. The bride wore a white dress that day, with a chartreuse print in the style of Marimekko, and a white, wide-brimmed hat that my uncle sported for most of the reception in the back yard. The groom wore a grey suit, and an enormous smile.

I was the Maid of Honor, and rumor has it that I dropped an F-bomb at some point during the ceremony, it's unclear whether that was before or after the photo was taken of me unceremoniously scratching my butt as they exchanged vows. Many of the guests graciously brought me birthday gifts, which delighted me of course, but in my mind I was already the luckiest girl in the world — I mean, how many kids get a dad for their fifth birthday? And as our family evolved, I internalized a truth that would ultimately lead me to my own children:

Love is independent of genetics.

∽

I grew up in a bubble. I didn't realize that at the time, of course — like most kids, I assumed the rest of the world functioned according to the same laws that governed my own, rooted in the ethos of *Sesame Street*, with the soundtrack of *Free to Be You and Me* floating in the background.

Our new house was in a neighborhood called The Back Lot, which resembled a slightly wonky tic tac toe board in its layout — four alleys crisscrossed the block, and houses were wrapped around the perimeter, with a communal park in the center that was maintained by the surrounding homeowners. One side of the park held a big field with a baseball diamond, and a basketball court which the parents would spray with water in the winter, converting it into an ice skating rink. There was a bench nearby where we would catch our breath in-between rounds of kickball or capture-the-flag, and where the teenagers (we called them The Benchies) would hang out after dark doing Mysterious Teenager-Things.

On the other side of the park was an impossibly high swingset, fashioned from heavy steel pipes with four low slung seats suspended by thick chains that would pinch your fingers if you weren't careful. There, we would take turns propelling each other skyward — shouting "Underdog!" as we ran underneath the swingee with our final push, hoping to successfully dodge a sneaker to the head. Behind it stood another steel pipe structure, but instead of swings it held two trapeze bars and a set of rings, the perfect setting for our Olympic competitions — which always involved extensive negotiations over who would be Olga Korbut and who would be Nadia Comaneci. There were climbing structures and a covered sandbox and a set of toddler swings too, and a tall aluminum slide that we would prime with wax paper before careening down, to land in a pile of sand at the bottom.

Every family had a unique signal of some kind to call the kids home when it was time for dinner — Heidi's mom rang a cowbell, Jesse's blew a trumpet. Brad's mom would strike a gong, Ruthie's would shake a wooden clacker brought home from a trip to Mexico. Our dinner bell was a heavy iron triangle. It hung just outside the back door, and the rule was that we could go anywhere within hearing range, and we had ten minutes to get home after being summoned. So we would play Ghost in the Graveyard and endless rounds of Sardines. We would have water balloon fights or snowball fights, depending on the season. We would jump on our bikes and ride down the alley to the next block, where someone had set up a makeshift candy store in their garage, and exchange handfuls of coins pilfered from between couch cushions for Bazooka Joe bubble gum and and those candy cigarettes that would release a puff of sugar dust when you blew into them which looked like real smoke. It made us feel quite sophisticated when we lined up on the bench, posing as The Benchies.

In my bubble, racism was ancient history — a horrifying chapter of our country's past that had finally been resolved with the Civil Rights Movement. The majority of our neighbors were white, yes, but there were also families of various skin tones and religious beliefs and cultural practices. And as far as I could tell, no one gave it a second thought. I certainly didn't. I didn't understand, yet, how ignoring our differences rather than exploring them just increases the space between us, reinforces our ignorance, blunts our compassion. I repeated the phrase "I don't see color" with righteous pride, blind to the fact that I might as well be saying "I don't see *you*". I cringe to think of it now.

In my bubble, sexism was ancient history, too — women were empowered. No longer relegated to the kitchen and the nursery, we could do anything (as long as we were home in time to make dinner). Not only *could* we "have it all", we were expected to *want* to "have it all", and to *strive* to "have it all". It was the time of Ms. Magazine, and those pervasive Enjoli perfume ads with a beautiful woman alternating between a bathrobe, a business suit, and a sexy negligee while she sings to the rhythm of an exotic dancer:

"I can put the wash on the line," ... *Daaa na na...*

"Feed the kids, get dressed, pass out the kisses, and get to work by five-of-nine," ... *Daaa na na...*

"Cause I'm a woooman," ... *Enjoli...*

"I can bring home the bacon," ... *Daaa na na...*

"Fry it up in a pan," ... *Daaa na na...*

"And never never never let you forget you're a man,"

"Cause I'm a woooman," ... *Enjoli...*

Male voiceover:

"Give her Enjoli, the eight hour perfume for the twenty-four hour woman."

The twenty-four hour woman — that was the bar. It felt like a big responsibility.

It was painful when I began to outgrow my childhood sphere, to glimpse the rest of the world as it actually was, governed by its own set of laws. I remember the shock, as a teenager, of hearing another teenager use a racial slur, and my reflexive response, "Hey — you can't talk to him like that!"

"Sara, shush!" my friend Nancy had whispered harshly, grabbing my arm. "You don't know what that guy might do." The bus was pulling up to our stop, and she hustled me onto the sidewalk as soon as the doors opened.

"I just can't believe that someone our age could think like that," I was dumbfounded, shaking with fury, "I mean, it's bad enough from an old person who was raised in ignorance, but we know better!"

The bubble was beginning to leak.

7

FIRST SPRING

That first spring after JJ died, I dreamt of a newborn joey. No bigger than a lima bean, shaped like one too. A translucent red lima bean, veins visible beneath the thin sheath of cells containing the unformed beginnings of a life. Scant protection from the elements, certainly. A bean sized sac with nothing but two tiny arms — suddenly expelled into the world and expected to find its way to safety, unaided. If it slips off during its journey, it will tumble to the ground and languish there, fated never to fulfill its destiny. The stakes are high. I am terrified. Helpless. I watch as the tiny arms reach out, one over the other, grabbing and pulling, grabbing and pulling, naked and blind, but guided by some ancient knowledge toward its destiny. It cannot stop, it will succeed or it will die.

Disoriented. Disorganized. Dismembered. I was feeling my way through with the tips of my nerves, each point of contact shocking and nearly unbearable. My senses were overloaded, and thus shut down to all but the most imminent facets of moving through the day. Every single moment required my complete concentration in order to process, interpret, and adapt to this new state. It was exhausting. I was capable of doing exactly one thing at a time, and very slowly at that. *I'm rinsing the dishes... now I'm putting them in the dishwasher... now I'm turning it on — wait, put in the soap...* like walking through jello. For months.

I was compelled to keep moving, towards what I did not know. I only knew that I had to hold on tight to my sons. Even when they pushed away — tighter then — because I could not let them fall. Could not let them slip beyond my reach. Could not let them languish there. I could not stop. They would succeed, or I would die.

At some point during that time I watched a show in which the main character had lost her fiancee, and she was devastated. She asked a wise old woman how she could possibly go on, to which the wise woman replied, "You just do dear. You just keep on living, until one day, you start to feel alive again."

Grabbing and pulling, grabbing and pulling, grabbing and pulling...

～

"That's not how Daddy does it." The phrase that accompanied every new task I attempted to master. "Daddy puts peanut butter on both pieces of bread with the jam in the middle so it doesn't make the bread all soggy." "Daddy doesn't tuck my sheet in on the side cause he knows my feet need to breathe." "Daddy gets the bubble bath that doesn't sting our eyes." It was weeks before they switched to the past tense.

"Dad would've been a chaperone for Outdoor School," Culby said quietly as he pulled the packet of papers out of his backpack.

"I know Culbs," I swallowed hard against the lump in my throat. "Would you ever want me to come?" I tried to decipher his face but it was so hard to read, "I mean I don't even know if they'd let me since we couldn't stay in the same cabin, but I can ask…"

"But what about Charlie?" He looked up at me quickly, his brow creased with concern, "It's for three whole days."

"He could stay with Meg and Brian," I said. It was tricky finding the right balance — being present for them without shining a spotlight right on the empty space where their dad should be, "I'd love to go if you want me to, but it's also totally fine if you don't."

"Well, okay… yeah, you can ask."

That's about as much enthusiasm as I was gonna get. *I'll take it!*

I was in charge of the Cougar cabin (a bit on the nose, no doubt). It was a sturdy little A-frame with built in cedar bunkbeds lining the walls, that sat at the far end of the camp just over a tiny bridge that was exactly two steps long.

Over the next three days we hunted insects to classify by order and species, analyzed the mineral content of the nearby stream, learned about the ancient fossils unearthed in the surrounding desert, and studied the life cycle of the lizards that hid among the juniper and sagebrush. Culby and I had an epic tickle war that stretched out over the whole three days, and we quickly mastered the stealth attack. Mindful of the sun's location after the Great Shadow Showdown of Day One, and having recruited allies on both sides of the battle, we staged a series of multi-pronged tickle

incursions on the treacherous routes between classes. We
showed no mercy.

After dinner we collected our flashlights and hiked up
to the highest point, where a telescope waited, holding the
whole sky in its convex lens. Culby and I were excited, we
were hoping to see the constellation Pegasus, and the star
my dad had named for JJ. It's only visible late at night, and
only during certain times of the year. When you register the
name they send you a photo of the star and its neighbors,
and they ask if you want anything printed on the image, so
my dad had asked the boys what we should say. They
thought for a long minute, and then Charlie said slowly,
"How about, *As long as your star shines we can always find
our way home.*" My dad and I exchanged looks. Sometimes
there's nothing else to say.

We didn't find JJ's star that night, a veil of clouds hid
him from us. Culby was stoic, "It doesn't matter, it's not like
it's really him anyway," he said softly as we finally turned to
leave. The longing for his dad was tangible, though, his pain
so enormous my arms couldn't reach all the way around it.
No matter how hard I searched for a way in, for a path that
would lead me to the very core of his suffering so that I
could absorb it, lift it from him, give him back his
innocence... I was impotent. I could only walk beside him.
Like with his father before him. I couldn't fix it.

～

The next week was Information Night at the middle school
where Culby would be starting sixth grade the following
fall. It was conveniently located one block from our house,
and the three of us walked up together in the evening light.
This would be our first transition as a tricycle. We had

talked about how strong and stable a tricycle is, how far it can go if the wheels are all working together and the frame is solid, but how if one wheel comes loose the whole unit needs to stop and fix it before moving forward again. If one or the other of us was having a hard day or a "Daddy Moment" Charlie would look at me and say, "Mom, I think we have a wonky wheel."

There were bleachers lining one side of the gymnasium, and chairs arranged on the floor for the band to play. The fifth graders gathered in clumps at the very top of the bleachers and Culby joined them while Charlie and I found a spot farther down with the other parents. I'd gotten to know a few of them over the last months as I'd tried to step into JJ's shoes, saying "Yes!" to every volunteer opportunity at the school, but I was a mystery to many of them before JJ died, and now I was his *Poor Widow*. I hated being tragic.

Charlie played on my phone and I focused on breathing while we sat on the grooved metal bench listening to speeches and presentations and performances. I was grateful for the friend who came and sat next to me, grateful to be able to quietly release the words that festered in the back of my throat, "This is so hard," grateful for her kind hug. When it was over, the boys and I walked back home together, and tightened up our wheels.

～

I somehow made it through all the things that come with spring in elementary school — the plays and band performances, the picnics and parades, the fundraisers and field trips. I learned to always carry a tissue and stopped wearing mascara.

There's a lovely tradition for the graduating fifth-graders at our elementary school called the Clap Out. On the last day of school, all of the students and teachers line the hallways leading to the gymnasium where the parents form a tunnel with their arms raised overhead, fingers clasped with a corresponding parent's across the aisle. Then all the fifth graders run down the hall and through the tunnel to the stage while everyone claps and cheers them on. It's fun and festive and loud.

It was a surreal day. Most of me was there, filled with love and pride, clapping and cheering like all the other parents, giving Culby a high-five when he ran through the tunnel. But a piece of me floated apart from the rest, I could sense it just beyond my peripheral vision. It floated there, observing how wrong it all was because it should have been JJ's hands I held as we formed the tunnel, not a random stranger's. Noting every moment where he should have been, every hoot that was not his, every missing hug.

To celebrate we went to Oaks Park, Portland's miniature amusement park with rides and bumper cars and mini golf; there's a roller rink, too, where the championship women's roller derby team, The Rose City Rollers is headquartered. It was popular among the under-twelve set, and the last place I wanted to spend an afternoon, but I had over-compensation down to an art now, I could handle it.

The boys weren't tall enough to go on the biggest rides yet, but we spent hours on the Scrambler and the Tilt-A-Whirl and the Spider. Charlie hated the powerlessness of Zero Gravity, Culby was thrilled by the Tree Top Drop. We rode the Oaks Park Train and raced Go Karts. We ate junk food and made silly faces in the photo booth. Moments of joy caught me off guard, they were difficult to recognize, they looked different. Always with a shadow now.

In the car on the way home I was thirsty and asked Culby for a sip of the water I'd gotten him before we left, he declined. "Are you kidding me?" I was suddenly, irrationally, furious, "After a day of getting literally everything you wanted, you can't even give me a sip of water?" I flashed him a dark look in the rearview mirror. His mouth was slightly open and his eyes were wide with surprise.

"Ummm... here you go Mom," he leaned forward from the back seat, offering me the bottle.

"Never mind," I huffed, "I don't even want it now." It was quiet for a minute while I marinated in my fury, and then Culby popped the tension with a well aimed observation.

"Mom," he said calmly, "I think you're being kind of passive aggressive." At which point, I nearly flipped my lid... but I took a deep breath instead, and then we all burst out laughing — because of course he was right, I was such a hypocrite! Passive aggression makes me crazy, and I've lectured them numb on the art of respectful self-advocacy, on the importance of communication and the perils of assumption. It dawned on me that afternoon that my sons would continue to keep me connected and accountable no matter what — they would always call me on my shit, and for that I was deeply grateful. Because without JJ to help me see beyond myself, I worried I might wither into one of those unfortunate souls who grows myopic in their loneliness, unable to see the magic in the kaleidoscope of perspectives. Lost in a house of mirrors.

∾

With spring came another string of Firsts: First Mother's Day, First Father's Day, my First birthday, our First anniversary... a string of hard days, days to be survived. With an occasional bright flash in between, lighting the way toward summer. Summer in the Pacific Northwest — JJ's happy place. Summer meant camping and fishing and kayaking and white water rafting. Hiking and biking and picnics. Music festivals and berry picking and Family Dinners on the deck. I was panicked at the thought of it.

8

PHYSICS 101

(1997-2003)

J J and I met in Portland, on a beautiful early summer day in 1997, at a dog funeral. I was bald. Not shiny-head bald, more like 5:00 shadow. It was the result of a lice infestation that would not be tamed despite gallons of Guatemalan insecticide which left burns on my scalp, but didn't bother the lice even a little bit. The only thing left to do was shave it. And as it turns out, I have a surprisingly small head. But on the upside, it was pretty low maintenance.

We were there to honor Bailey, my roommate's 120 pound Rottweiler and Kan's best buddy. Bailey had defended our house from a would-be-thief by jumping through the big bay window in the living room and chasing him away — by all accounts an amusing scene which would have made an entertaining tale if it hadn't ended so tragically. Bailey was understandably agitated and paced the perimeter of the lawn, but he never left the property, so our neighbor was horrified when the police arrived and opened with, "You know, we could just shoot it now and be done with it."

"NO! That's not why I called you! He's a great dog, he's just all worked up and I'm nervous to try and get him into the back yard by myself!" The poor guy was completely distraught. And he only grew more so as he watched the police escalate the situation. We learned later that the officers had received no training in animal management despite their obligation to cover for Animal Control after hours or on the weekend, and they succeeded only in riling Bailey up even more. At one point, an officer had a steak of some kind and was attempting to lure Bailey into the squad car by waiving it around before tossing it onto the back seat. It's not clear what happened next, but there was a scuffle, and Bailey was shot at least twice, the final time as he desperately clawed at the mudroom door, wounded, and trying to get to safety.

When my roommate arrived home around ten that Friday night, she found a gaping hole where the window had been, and a small piece of paper tacked to the front door that read "Your dog escaped and was shot and killed. Call this number on Monday to collect his body." She was shattered.

JJ and Brian had moved to Portland together after college from the flatlands of the midwest, to the mountains and the snow, and they worked with my roommate at a cozy little pizza place that was all dark wood and craft beers, where people gathered and played boardgames while they ate. When she introduced us, I was instantly taken with the blue of JJ's eyes and the ease of his laugh, the comfortable way he wore his skin. I felt an electric tingle in my core when he touched my arm.

But I was stuck in the final throes of a fading romance just then, I couldn't lean in. Yet.

· · ·

Two months later, I felt a tap on my shoulder. I was sitting in Physics 101, my hair growing in with two swirling cowlicks in back and a peak along the top that gave me the look of a recently electrocuted chicken.

"You're Sara, right? Jenny's roommate?" JJ was sitting right behind me. "I recognized your head," he added with a grin.

Later, he offered to help me wrap my head around the concept of wave-particle duality — which he already understood since he'd taken physics as an undergraduate and was just re-taking some classes before applying to graduate school — and I happily accepted. I really did need some help, but if I'm honest, it was mostly because of the twinkle in his denim-blue eyes when he laughed.

It was meant to be a fling. At 24, he was far too young for me (I had just turned 30, after all) and anyway, he was only in Portland for three more months...

Sometimes life has other plans.

≈

I knew I loved him the day I lost his dog. Her name was Sinjin. She was a black and tan Australian Shepherd, a gift for him from his little sister Kate, and the runt of her litter. When he first brought her home, she was so small she could sit on the palm of his hand, a tiny ball of fluff with a face. Freaking adorable. Kan thought so too, and would stand patiently while Sinjin circled him at full speed, running around and around, herding his legs like they were four errant sheep. When he wanted to move, he would look down, and with perfect timing, pin the flying fluff ball with his paw and then pick her up gently in his mouth. If he was thirsty, for example, he would carry her over to the water bowl and set her down beside him, where she would shake herself off and then resume her laps while he had a drink. At first we thought Sinjin was a savant, we marveled at how quickly she learned to Sit, Lie Down, Stay — I was exceedingly impressed with JJ's dog-training skills. But, then we realized that it actually had nothing to do with us. She just did whatever Kan did.

"Are you sure you trust me with her?" I asked, when he brought her to my house at dawn one day, "I mean, she's just a baby." JJ laughed his easy laugh and set her down next to Kan, who promptly picked her up in his mouth and took her out to the back yard where she immediately got to work herding him.

"Of course I trust you," he said. "Thank you for taking care of her, she's just too little to climb Mount Saint Helen's yet. I thought about bringing her in my backpack, but we're snowboarding down, and that just doesn't feel safe." He kissed me goodbye, and then I brought both dogs in from the back yard and firmly closed the door — there were a few openings in the fence that a tiny puppy might squeeze through, and I was not about to risk that.

"Keith," I called to my current roommate (Jenny couldn't bear being in the house after Bailey was killed, and had moved out shortly after the funeral. My new roommate was... interesting... he liked to brew beer in our bathtub, and for some reason refused to erase any voicemails from our house phone, regardless of who the message was from or for — and he would get very upset with me if I deleted one. I'm still not sure what that was about), "Please be sure to keep the doors closed — JJ's new puppy is here for a couple of days and we can't let her escape."

"Okay," he mumbled from his bedroom.

Twenty minutes later I walked into the kitchen, and the door to the back yard was standing wide open.

I need a new roommate, I thought as I rushed outside to find Kan lying on the grass, asleep in the morning sun. Sinjin was nowhere in sight.

"Sinjin," I called, waking Kan up from his nap as I scoured the small yard. It didn't take long, there weren't many places to hide, "Come here good girl!" Then my eyes landed on a puppy sized hole along the bottom of the fence, leading to the front of the house and the street, and I started to panic. "Sinjin!" I called, louder now, as I ran through the house and out the front door, Kan at my heels. I fought a growing sense of desperation as we searched behind bushes and under cars, my voice steadily rising in pitch and volume, "Sinjin! Come good girl!" I felt a lump forming in my throat and tears filling my eyes, when it suddenly struck me — JJ was probably still packing up the car — and I took off, running the half-mile to his house, barefoot and still in my pajamas. I was breathless and verging on hysterical when I arrived.

"JJ!" I cried when I found him in the driveway organizing his gear, "I... lost... Sinjin..." I was weeping so thoroughly by then that each word required its own short intake of breath, making the rest of my explanation mostly unintelligible. JJ set down the backpack he was holding and quietly wrapped his arms around me.

My heart rate instantly slowed, my breathing calmed, and when I stopped shaking, he leaned back and smiled serenely, "It's okay," he said softly, sweeping away my tears with his thumb. "Don't worry, we'll find her."

My heart expanded in that moment, reached out and wrapped itself around his.

We did find Sinjin, and by we, I mean Kan. He found

her curled up behind the woodpile stacked against the back wall of my house, where she had apparently discovered a tiny little nook and decided to take a nap. She'd never even left the yard.

Not long after that, Keith moved out. And JJ moved in. Sinjin too, of course.

~

We moved to Seattle in 1999, when I started medical school at the University of Washington, and it's only in hindsight that I fully grasp what a sacrifice that was for JJ. How hard it must have been to find himself in a strange city, away from all of his friends, with a partner who was completely immersed in studying and frequently unavailable. And we weren't even engaged yet. But I can only imagine how that must have felt, because he never once complained.

Nor did he complain that New Year's Eve when we went to Mexico with some friends to celebrate the end of the century, and I was, let's just say, not my best self. I don't even remember why I was so prickly, but I do confess that I could be a bit moody sometimes, and I cringe when I recall him cajoling me into a sunset walk on the beach, and my tart response, "Okay, *fine*," probably accompanied by a loud sigh and a dramatic roll of the eyes. He just smiled his sanguine smile, taking my hand and leading me down to the ocean, where he dropped to one knee, and asked me to be his wife.

"But... I've been such a raging bitch all day," I said, stunned.

"That's how I know we'll be okay," he said, looking up at me with a smile. "Because I love you Doll, all of you. And I want to marry you, even on your very worst day."

≈

Shortly after we were engaged, JJ decided to travel to Guatemala. For three months. On his own.

"Because the time you spent there is such an important part of who you are," he explained. "I feel like I need to experience a little bit of it myself."

He explored the jungle and the highlands and the Rio Dulce. He spent time in places I'd never even been, and in places I still treasure. He studied Spanish and spent time with my friends, collecting other travelers, too, that he met along the way. He saw my little open-air apartment in Antigua, with the giant red pila, the old maid's quarters from when the whole block was a single house. He ate black bean and avocado sandwiches from the Bread Lady who opened her doors across from the ruins of La Merced every morning at 10, closing them again when the day's stock ran out. And he listened to poetry and guitar music around the fire at the Rainbow Reading Room, which had been my mailing address for the time I'd lived there.

He was right, that trip did deepen our understanding of each other. Strengthened our foundation. It gave him a glimpse into my past, and it gave me a glimpse into our future.

≈

I adored everything about our wedding day, but I was dreading the First Dance. To us, dancing meant moving your body in random ways to some sort of rhythm; waltzing and orchestrated twirls were simply not in our repertoire. So in an effort not to humiliate ourselves, we decided to take a class at a nearby studio. It did not end well. I can't even remember what the argument was about, but by the end, I was in tears, and JJ had vowed never to take another dancing class with me. I resigned myself to three-and-a-half minutes of mortification.

So when he took me in his arms and floated me around the dance floor on our wedding day, guiding me with gentle assurance and never once stepping on my toes, I was stunned. He even managed to make it look like I knew what I was doing, such was his grace.

"J, what *was* that?" I was flabbergasted, "Where did that come from?"

"Well," he grinned, "I said I'd never take another dancing lesson *with you*. I didn't say anything about going on my own."

~

As I was finishing up medical school, JJ was being courted by graduate programs. He'd decided to pursue a PhD in Biotechnology, and it was his turn now. So in 2003, when he accepted a spot at Washington State University in Pullman, Washington, we moved to Spokane, about 75 miles north, where I would do my last few clinical rotations, and then Residency. Before I could join JJ there though, I had to complete my pediatrics rotation and then a month in the Emergency Department of the County Hospital, so I stayed behind in Seattle at first.

One morning during that transition period, probably around five, I was getting ready for a day at the Children's Hospital, when I saw Kan standing at the bottom of the basement stairs. "C'mon Kan," I called, "Let's go for a walk!" But instead of bounding up the stairs and collecting a ball (or three) to take along, as was his way, he just stood there looking up at me. Sinjin had appeared at my side, ready to go as soon as she'd heard the word *walk*, but Kan made no move to come up from the basement. "Come on buddy, let's go!" I didn't have time for games, I needed to get to the hospital and see my patients before my attending physician arrived for rounds. I watched as Kan slowly raised one paw, placing it on the bottom step, and looked back up at me. He couldn't climb the stairs.

I flew down to him, my heart in my throat, and started checking for injuries. There was nothing obvious; we had been camping the previous weekend, and he had been running and swimming and playing the whole time, maybe he was just sore? Regardless, I needed to get him out of the basement, and the only way out was up. I moved around behind him, and placed his two front paws on a step, one by one. Then I pushed his haunches and helped guide his hind legs up a step, keeping my body behind his rump so that he didn't slide back down to the bottom. Then we did it again. And again. Step by agonizing step. By the time we got to the top, I was covered in sweat and we were both panting.

I remembered where the Emergency Vet was, from the time Kan got a racquetball lodged in his throat, but couldn't get him into my car by myself so I ran next-door and woke my neighbor, frantically ringing the bell and banging on the door until a light switched on, and he appeared in the doorway, glasses and hair equally askew. "I need your help — something's wrong with Kan and JJ's not here and I can't get him into my car alone, please come help me!"

The Vet was kind, "I'm sorry," he said gently.

Bloody fluid had filled the sack that surrounded Kan's heart, constricting it, rendering its beats feeble and ineffectual. There was a tumor in the blood vessels, which had grown tangled and misshapen, prone to leakage and rupture, so that any volume removed would be quickly replaced. There was nothing to be done. I was devastated.

I dashed back to the house to collect Sinjin so she and Kan could have a last moment together, and when she saw him, lying on his side on a thin cushion in a corner of the exam room, panting, she ran over and lay down beside him, and began licking the corner of his mouth, an affectionate habit she'd picked up as a puppy. I sat on the floor, Kan's head in my lap, and wept.

Endings, and beginnings.

$\sim$

Our move to eastern Washington was only temporary, we would return to Portland to start our careers once we finished our training. And we would also begin working toward our dream — to create a health and education center in Guatemala.

Sometimes life has other plans.

9

AN ASIDE

L est I leave you with the impression that I always
have my rose colored glasses firmly in place when
reflecting on JJ, or that he must actually be a
figment of my imagination because nobody is *that* great, let
me assure you that he was indeed a whole person, and flawed
just like the rest of us. We had our share of frustrations and
arguments, of misunderstandings and hurt feelings and even
moments of fury with each other — it took us four and a half
years to figure out how to fight without leaving wounds.

The thing is, when I try to slip past the emotion of those
moments and remember *why* we actually argued, I struggle
to get there. I can recall the feelings, but the details are
elusive. Perhaps that's because in the grand scheme of
things, they're just so insignificant that I can't quite believe I
cared.

JJ never wiped down the kitchen counters, for example.
He would clean the whole kitchen, but for some reason he
would never wipe down the damn counters, and it drove me
mad. They were that crazy granite from the early 2000s, the

busy kind that camouflages everything, and I remember picking up the signature page of a form I needed to sign for work, and leaving half of it glued to the counter by a glob of jam. I was furious.

And the laundry. I almost left him over a beautiful cashmere sweater that came out of the dryer small enough to fit a toddler. Did I mention it was cashmere? And that he put it in the dryer?

Frequently, he would plan dinner in the morning, and then leave all of the non-perishable ingredients along with whatever cookware would be required, out on the counter for the whole day. It was so annoying.

Often, I got frustrated when I would come home after a long shift at the hospital and the house was a mess. It was clean underneath the clutter, but still, there was always *stuff* everywhere.

Sometimes, JJ would subscribe to the "Easier to beg for forgiveness than ask for permission" credo — which was exasperating. Like the time I came home to find an enormous television mounted to our bedroom wall, "It was on sale Doll, I don't think I can take it back. Plus, there are some holes in the wall now..."

Occasionally, something would get under his skin for reasons that remained mysterious to me. Like the time he got obsessed with the fact that a realtor had put an Open House sign, for a house up the street, on our lawn without asking — and I do mean obsessed. To this day I do not know why it bothered him so much, but he was furious and he could not let it go. It could ruin an entire evening if I missed the moment to redirect the conversation.

And once, he yelled at me in the middle of a dinner party. I was *livid*. I don't even remember what he was so roiled about, but I distinctly recall that I was right, and he was wrong.

The thing is, it was all just so meaningless. So trivial. So silly. I mean, perhaps I could have appreciated the fact that he cleaned the whole kitchen instead of focusing on the jammy counters. I have hands and access to a sponge after all. And he literally did all the laundry, maybe I could have put my dry cleaning in a separate spot so he knew not to ruin it. I could choose to focus on the annoyance of spice jars and produce bags on the kitchen counter, or I could be grateful for the lovely dinner waiting for me when I got home late at night and everyone else was already in bed. And as for the *stuff* everywhere, it turns out the bulk of it was mine, and JJ didn't want to put it away because I would then be annoyed when I couldn't find my things. We all have our quirks, our irrational moments, our labyrinthine triggers, and the blending of two lives is always complicated, even under the best of circumstances.

The gift that cancer gave us, was perspective. That, and the opportunity to choose.

10

FIRST SUMMER

"**A**re you sure you can handle it Mom?" Culby stood in the kitchen, arms crossed, assessing the state of our camping gear with a skeptical look on his face.

"Oh I will handle the *shit* out of it — you just watch."

"But you never do anything," Culby said. *Ouch,* I thought.

He wasn't buying it, "Every time, Dad packs up the whole car, and then when we get there, he brings you your red chair and a Pacifico, and he sets everything up by himself." I had to laugh — it was true. It was also true that JJ and I were fans of yellow beer, his loyalty lay with PBR while I preferred a Mexican vintage.

"Yeah," Charlie chimed in, "do you even know how to put up the tent?" Well, now I was offended.

"First of all," I said indignantly, "just because you haven't *seen* me do something doesn't mean I *can't*. I am perfectly capable of *handling* a camping trip. It's not like I didn't try to help. Daddy wouldn't let me. Do you want to know why?"

"Yeeeeesss!" They lit up at any opportunity to hear a new story about their dad.

"Because he loved it, so he wanted me to love it too, and I didn't grow up camping — I mean, can you imagine the Grandies in a tent?" We looked at each other and cracked up at the idea of my parents wrestling their way into a sleeping bag, "So when we started dating and he took me camping it was his rule that I was never allowed to do any of the work."

"Never?"

"Never. Not for 20 years. One time, we hiked eight miles in to a remote little hot springs on Vancouver Island and he wouldn't even let me carry my own backpack — he strapped his on his back and mine on his front." This left them duly impressed with their father's virility, and no less skeptical of my skills.

There were two big bins labeled "Camping" along with half a dozen sleeping bags of various shapes and sizes, a collection of outdoor cookware including a cast iron pot that weighed more than either of my children, and a variety of foldable furniture — some of which had clearly been designed by a sadist with a sense of humor. There were five tents ranging in size from individual to hotel, a stack of tarps with multicolored ropes for mysterious purposes still tied to their stainless grommets, and several long bags holding poles and stakes of unclear attachment.

As gear goes, we had some.

A frequent refrain in our house went like this:

"Babe, why is there a snowboard / bicycle / kayak in the living room?"

"I found it on Craig's list, Doll — it was a steal!"

"But why? Don't we already have six snowboards / bicycles / kayaks?"

"Just in case, you never know..." Wink.

I opened the first bin, and immediately closed it again. I took a deep breath. *I can do this. I got this. I can do this.* I cracked it open and peeked inside. Right on top were two ziplock bags, one with several flashlights and the other with the corresponding batteries. "You never want to store them with the batteries *in,* Doll," I heard him say. He had labeled each of them with a black sharpie in his distinctive hand — *NOPE can't do it.* I snapped it shut again, but the smell of campfire had already crept into the room, teasing me with flashes of hammocks and beach chairs and trash mags. Of friendship and music and laughter. Of oysters with tabasco and paella for 50, Picklebacks and homemade Fireball, surfboards and paddle boards and glow-in-the-dark bocce. Forts in the woods and castles on the beach.

Our camping crew had grown with us over the years. Expanded as our lives did, to encompass partners and children and a variety of dogs. We were a dozen or so families by then, and Cape Lookout was our communal Happy Place. It sits on a long spit that separates a marshy bay to the east from the vast Pacific to the west. The three group campsites were separated from the general campground and, combined, were big enough to hold all of us. We would set our chairs along the ridge that looked over the beach and the crashing waves, and the kids would scramble down the rocky slope to the sand. Behind us was an old growth forest, ripe for exploration, adventure, and the construction of elaborate hammock villages. Every winter we watched the minutes tick by until reservations opened, then dialed compulsively until someone sent out the message — "Got it!" Portions of the group would go for Memorial Day or Fourth of July, but everyone was always there for Labor Day, it was our End of Summer Celebration.

The year before, though, we had missed it. The boys and I were at City of Hope with JJ when we got a confusing photo from my cousin David (who's really more like a brother, to both JJ and me) that took us a minute to understand. It was an aerial view of the beach right in front of our campsite, with the blue sea on the left and the green forest on the right, and in the middle stretched out over the sand were two enormous Js. On closer inspection, the Js were made up of people lying head-to-toe, our people. "How did they do that?!" JJ and I exclaimed, and just then my phone dinged with another message from David, "Don't you want to know how we did that?" Ding. "Rachel marked it out and then lined everyone up and Kurt went hang gliding with his camera — the timing was tricky, Rachel was herding drunk cats, but it worked!"

It did indeed.

I carried the bins out to the car as they were. Whatever we could possibly need would be there, probably in triplicate.

"I think we should sprinkle some Daddy at Cape Lookout," Charlie said, as he came into the living room where I was trying to figure out how exactly one stuffs an entire sleeping bag into a sack the size of a coffee cup.

"That's a great idea, sweetheart," I said, before giving up, and tossing the sleeping bag onto the cram-it-in-somewhere pile. "It was one of Daddy's favorite places."

"Yeah, we have lots of memories there," he said. "Plus, we know we'll always go back every year so we can visit him." We both smiled, it was a comforting thought.

When we camped, we usually teamed up with a couple of other families and took turns making dinner. I was profoundly intimidated by this because JJ took camp cooking to the next level. He made coq au vin in that cast iron pot set over the campfire, carne asada with grilled scallions and perfect margaritas (we ate pretty late that night), Philly cheesesteaks with lightly toasted buns, and individual pies baked over the fire in long handled cooking irons for dessert. All of which fell far beyond my skill set, but I was determined to honor him by not resorting to hot dogs, so I spent days cooking homemade spaghetti sauce and sautéing vegetables for morning scrambles. I soaked cinnamon sticks wrapped in cheesecloth in a glass jar of whiskey then seasoned it with homemade chili oil, and squeezed a dozen pink grapefruits by hand. I had every imaginable snack and a separate cooler for drinks. I was ready.

My heart skipped a beat as we pulled up to the ranger station to register like we had so many times before, except that I had never been the driver, never been the one to hop out and chat for a minute with the ranger while they wrote out our parking pass, never been the one to drive down the dirt road toward the beach, turning left where the main road went right, parking along the row of familiar cars — not too close to the port-o-potties. There were already several tents up and several more in progress, a growing line of chairs along the ridge, a tapped keg on ice. Music played and dogs sniffed each other in greeting, kiddos assessed the state of the forest and the beach, hunting for relics of past weekends. A wave of emotion rose up, from my belly straight to my eyes which promptly overflowed. But that was okay. We were safe here in our sacred spot, surrounded by friends who lost him too, who loved him too, who held us in our grief. It was a relief. I took a deep breath.

And I *did* handle the shit out of that camping trip, if I do say so myself. With a little help from JJ's bins.

On our last afternoon we walked back into the woods, to our favorite tree. It was a massive cedar, one of the tallest in the forest with elegant limbs stretching out and curving forward slightly, inviting you in to its embrace. Charlie, Culby and I each carried a small wine colored velvet pouch that held a handful of JJ's ashes, and we took turns sprinkling them at the base of the trunk. "We know you'll be happy here Daddy, see you at Labor Day!" We left a PBR there, too, just in case.

～

In retrospect, that summer was a lot. In the spirit of keeping us distracted, I had manically filled the calendar, fearful of empty days and sleepless nights, spent imagining what we would be doing *if only*.... so we traveled around the country visiting family, and in between trips we packed up the camping gear again and headed to our favorite music festival, or as my kids called it, "The Land of Unicorns and Rainbows".

There, when you arrived you were directed to a huge field and a spot among the rows of dusty cars, which would sit untouched for the duration. If this was not your first time, you knew to bring a wagon to haul your camping gear along the dirt trail and up into the woods where everybody pitched their tents (one year JJ and I had arrived late and had to pitch ours high up on the hill at such a slant that we slept with our feet propped on a cooler propped on a tree, to avoid sliding down into our neighbor's sleeping bag). You would also know that the shoes you wore would be sacrificial and that within 30 seconds of exiting your car you would be covered with a fine layer of dirt that would continue to accumulate throughout the coming days. You would embrace it.

As you made your way along the dirt trail you would pass open-air tents housing face painters and puppeteers, perhaps dodge a unicycler or someone walking on stilts, and as you rounded the bend you might see a friend working in the swag tent, another driving a golf cart filled with musicians and their gear, (if your timing was good, they would even swing back after dropping the band off and give you a lift the rest of the way). As you continued up the trail you would come upon the Mount Hood Stage, set far back in an enormous field beyond a sky of intricately placed sail cloths that were distracting in their beauty and generous with their shade. Your stomach might growl when you smelled the deliciousness wafting out of the miniature versions of all your favorite Portland eateries off to the right of the stage, but you'd have to wait to unpack your plate first — no disposables allowed. And eventually you would arrive at the main trail ambling up into the woods, with dozens of arteries spreading out among the trees, all lined with fairy lights and leading to pop up neighborhoods made up of like-minded souls.

There were five other stages scattered over the 88 acre farm, each one unique for its individual setting and acoustics, cherished for its memories. The music was always an eclectic mix of artists and genres, and played from the early morning through the wee hours of the night, replaced by drum circles and spontaneous jam sessions when the bands were spent.

It was a community of hundreds of people coming

together to celebrate music and friendship and summer. And the kids ruled it like benevolent overlords. They formed a pack, governed by two inviolable laws:

1) The Bigs look out for the Littles
2) No man left behind

Thus established, they roamed from show to show, stopping for free food and drinks from various vendors, "I don't know, someone's dad." They created their own micro-economy: After the wagons were unloaded they took them back to the parking area and made a fortune hauling gear up the bumpy trails; they drew pictures and sold them on the side of the paths leading to the various stages; they offered individual glow sticks to the starry eyed adults wandering between shows, for a dollar apiece. At some point they discovered that there was free soft-serve ice cream backstage for the musicians, and they figured out that if they just acted like they belonged there nobody questioned them. One night I realized it was 1:30am and though the Littles were fast asleep the Bigs were still out and about, "Brian, do you know what the kids are up to?"

"Yeah," he laughed, "I just talked to them, apparently they're hanging out backstage with the band."

I was grateful for this bubble, this safe happy place where we could set down our sorrow for a moment. Where we could believe that pure joy was still possible.

～

There were certain books that JJ didn't want me to read — the ones about adventures gone horribly, horribly wrong. People falling to their death while climbing a mountain for example, or anything by John Krakauer. Ever since Meg and I had almost called out a search party once, when he

and Brian were late returning from climbing Mount
Rainier, he'd made me promise that I would always wait at
least 24 hours because "I can survive anything for 24 hours,
Doll." He was good in a crisis.

This was on my mind the weekend after the music
festival as we set out in JJ's raft for the first time with Brian
as our captain now. We were taking a gentle float with the
kids down a mellow stretch of river that had one or two class
1 rapids — essentially ripples. It was a perfect August day,
the kind that gets you through the winter, with a sky so blue
it must be fake, and an occasional puffy white cumulus
cloud so elaborate you could spend all afternoon pulling
images from it. We had a cooler with drinks and snacks, a
giant blow up unicorn tied to the back of the raft, and Meg
was on her paddle board. People waved and shouted
greetings as they floated by on inner tubes and inflatable
islands, and we slathered on sunscreen as we pulled out into
the current. Nine-year-old Beau, Meg and Brian's middle
child, joined his mom on the paddle board, sitting at her feet
while she glided along. Brian steered the raft alongside
them.

"Look! An osprey!" shouted one of the kids. "No," said
another, "it's an eagle! See the tail?" We were all looking up
as we approached a bend in the river, so we hadn't noticed
Meg and Beau pulling ahead of us. They were already
rounding the curve out of sight when we heard Meg cry out
"BRIAN!" We heard the rush of the water before we saw
the rapid, "Class 1 my ass!" was Brian's assessment.

Meg and Beau were balanced precariously on a rock in
the middle of the river, surrounded by more rocks nosing up
through the torrents. They were struggling to hold on
against the force of the water. The paddle board flipped on
its side, the valve cap popped off, and the river rushed in,

sending it ricocheting off the serrated rocks and rushing around the bend up ahead — an ominous glimpse of the path Meg and Beau would take should they lose their grip. Brian struggled to steer the raft toward them but the current was indomitable, and as we drew parallel, it was clear we would not make it close enough to rescue them before being flung around the bend after the paddle board.

Then suddenly — we stopped.

Side by side, but 25 feet of churning whitewater away. The raft had caught on a rock that lay at the outer edge of the rapid, and we balanced there, holding our breath for fear we would come loose. Brian moved slowly, pulling the unicorn to the raft and grabbing ahold before gingerly maneuvering his right leg over the side, then his left. The unicorn threatened to escape but Brian held on tight as he found his balance and started across. When he slipped and disappeared for a moment, all four kids in the raft started to panic and I heard JJ in my ear, "Keep em calm, Doll."

"Okay guys," I tried to sound soothing, but had to shout over the noise of the rapid and probably ended up sounding more like an over-caffeinated librarian, "eyes on me — everybody take a big breath, in and out." We breathed together for a moment, "Our job right now is to stay totally still so we don't pop off this rock, okay?" Nods all around, "Brian's got this." He slipped and disappeared again, quickly popping back up, "See? And we can help him by staying calm so he can focus."

He had finally reached Meg and Beau and was using all his strength to hold the unicorn steady, while also remaining balanced upright on the slippery rocks against the force of the water, as they climbed on. Once they were on board he let go and they shot over the rapid, disappearing around the curve. Brian made his way back to us, safe but for some bumps and scrapes, and as we worked together to extract ourselves from our perch the kids all remained cool, calm and collected, following Brian's directions like pros — JJ would've been so proud.

Finally, we managed to get ourselves off the rocks without puncturing the raft, and as we followed their path around the bend, we spotted Meg and Beau on the shore with the unicorn, the paddle board, and the kayaker who had rescued them. "It's river etiquette, Doll," I heard JJ say, "of course he helped."

The water was smooth and glassy now, and once we'd collected them we drifted along in the gentle current, our adrenaline slowly ebbing. We marveled at the luck of getting stuck exactly where we needed to, at what good fortune it was that we'd brought the silly unicorn, at the kindness of the kayaker. "JJ was definitely watching over us," Brian said it. We all felt it.

Up ahead we saw a can bobbing in the river, someone must have dropped it accidentally — nobody would have tossed their rubbish into the water, people just didn't do that. Brian steered us toward it and as he fished it out to throw in with our recycling, a grin lit up his face, "Of course!" Turning toward us he held it up, a PBR.

～

The next weekend was Labor Day at Cape Lookout. Glorious and heartbreaking. The end of summer. The sun's warmth would thin, the clouds would coalesce, the rhythm of the days would shift. The time would come for homework and soccer and Back to School Night. For slippers and sweaters and school lunches, for PB&Js with peanut butter on both pieces of bread.

11

___

LASAGNA

(2004)

I t was February, 2004 in Spokane, where winter is real
and studded tires the norm. I was snuggled up under
the guest bed comforter surrounded by anatomy
textbooks when I heard JJ come in downstairs.

"Welcome home, Babe!" I called. I was always relieved
when he made it home safely from Pullman, especially in
the winter when invisible patches of black ice made the 90
minute drive especially treacherous.

"Babe?" Normally he came bounding up the stairs as
soon as he walked in the door, swept me up in an enormous
hug, and gave me a welcome respite from the intricacies of
the hepatobiliary system or the pathophysiology of
autoimmune disease. I smiled to myself, *He must have
something up his sleeve.*

"Hi Doll!" He sounded tired, and was slow coming up
the stairs.

Oh! He must be carrying something! In retrospect, I am
appalled at my self-absorption, my immediate assumption
that he was moving slowly because he was bringing me a
gift.

He paused as he reached the top of the stairs and turned to lean in the doorway, "I'm really tired Doll, I don't know why but I almost had to pull over — I thought I might fall asleep."

"What? Are you okay? Do you feel sick?"

"Nah, I'm okay. I feel better now. I'm gonna go get the..." his voice trailed off and I watched his face shift from confused to annoyed as he struggled to find the word, "the... you know... the thing that we keep in the freezer and you cook it for like an hour..."

"You mean the lasagna?"

"Yes! The lasagna!" Relief replaced annoyance and he smiled sheepishly, "Man, I need to eat some food and go to bed."

An hour later he called me for dinner, and I confess I did think it was a little odd that he'd made several unusually large and oddly misshapen biscuits to go with the lasagna, but we had a rule that the only thing we said when one of us cooked was "Thank you." It wasn't until much later that he told me he sat with the Bisquick box for 30 minutes trying to decipher the directions, which involved measuring out the Bisquick and the milk and then combining them. "It just didn't make sense, I couldn't figure out what I was supposed to do. I'd just decided to come and tell you something was wrong, but then it clicked and I got it." I raised an eyebrow, "I would've told you but I thought I was just tired..."

After dinner I went back to my books in the guest room so JJ could go to sleep, and a few hours later I was immersed in the natural history of sarcoidosis when I felt a jolt and Sinjin woke up, looking around anxiously. *That's a big truck to be going down our street this late at night.*

Sinjin disappeared briefly, and then came back — whining for me to follow her. She led me to our bedroom, and when I flipped on the light I was confused for a moment — JJ was not in the bed, but across the room face down on Sinjin's plush green pillow. Moaning.

"J, what happened? Are you OK?" I kneeled down and rolled him over. His five-o'clock shadow acted like velcro, pulling all of Sinjin's hair with it, giving him a long scraggly beard. He didn't seem to see me, his gaze was unfocused and wandering. He mumbled and pushed me away, struggling to get to his feet.

"JJ, what is happening?!" He groaned and waved his limbs around as if wondering who was in charge of them.

"I swear to God — if you're fucking with me you'd better tell me right now, because I'm calling 911!" I had already pressed 91. He continued mumbling as he lurched to his feet, knocking us both onto the bed. I hit the second 1.

(Now, I can see how accusing my husband of a poorly executed prank and screaming an expletive at him could be considered further evidence of my jackassery, but in all fairness when I told him about it later he responded with a chuckle, "Probably a good thing you checked, Doll.")

By the time the paramedics arrived he was coming around a bit. Confused and disoriented, but responsive at least. "Do you recognize this person?" The young EMT who was clearly in charge had a buzzcut that matched his no-nonsense demeanor.

"My wife... Sara." I was relieved, he'd had no idea a few minutes earlier.

"I think he had a seizure," I blurted out, "he's acting post-ictal."

"Did you witness any seizure activity?" Buzzcut was all business.

"No, but..." and I quickly explained what had happened. "I'm an Internal Medicine intern, so I know just enough to be annoying..." The corner of Buzzcut's mouth twitched in what almost looked like a fleeting grin.

After making sure he was stable, Buzzcut and his sidekick, Mullet, wrangled JJ into my car, no need for an expensive ambulance ride — the hospital was all of two miles away. And I knew that several of my friends were on duty in the ER. The only sound during the drive there was JJ saying over and over, like he was stuck on a loop, "Fuck, fuck, FUCK."

It's the oddest thing, I remember every detail of that night: the antiseptic smell of cleanser, the beeps and chimes of the busy ER, the squeak of the sweet janitor's shoes on the linoleum as he brought me a cup of intensely bitter coffee in a miniature styrofoam cup... I remember sitting on the hard beige plastic chair, holding JJ's hand waiting for test results, confident that we would be sent home soon with instructions to follow up with a neurologist, after all he was young and healthy and there was no reason to think there was anything seriously wrong. I remember steadfastly ignoring the voice in the the back of my head that kept taunting me, *tumor, tumor, tumor.*

And I remember the words that stopped the world: "There's an abnormality on the CT."

I remember going numb, my mind frozen in the space before those words, when I understood life and the world and it all made sense. And every moment of the long night that followed — MRI scan, anti-seizure medication, neurosurgery consult, more bloodwork, admission to the ICU. The phone calls to family, "Mom, I have a tumor in my head."

I remember waking up JJ's brother, who was also in graduate school at Washington State, and my deep relief when he appeared in the ICU to help me navigate. And the jolt that hit me when I realized that I had to be at our other hospital to meet my GI attending for a procedure in 30 minutes, and I was still in my flannel pajamas.

But when I try to picture the face of the incredibly kind doctor who said those words to us, all I see is a blank oval. I see the shape of his body, long and lean and comfortable in itself. I see his faded blue scrubs and his white coat with a coffee spill on the lapel, name tag clipped to the pocket, black wire readers poking out. I hear his voice, gentle and filled with genuine compassion. But when I started to write him a note to thank him for his care, I realized I had no idea who he was. Which was odd, because I knew him — I was a resident at that same hospital. But I could not, for the life of me, remember who it was that shattered our world.

After swapping my pajamas for some awkwardly oversized hospital scrubs, I left JJ in the ICU with his brother and dashed to the other hospital where I knew the Internal Medicine team would be meeting in the doctor's dining room for morning sign out. I needed some guidance, someone who knew more than I did, someone to help me navigate this Picasso painting we suddenly found ourselves in. I burst through the door unceremoniously and interrupted Dr. L in the middle of questioning another intern about an overnight admission.

"JJ's in the ICU — he had a seizure last night and they found a mass," my voice cracked. I was shaking, and suddenly lightheaded. Dr. L pulled out the chair next to her and patted it gently.

"Who was on call for neurosurgery?" Her face was creased with concern.

"Dr. E," seven months into an Internal Medicine residency I hadn't yet interacted with many of the neurosurgeons, and didn't know much about their reputations or technical skills, but the look on Dr. L's face spoke volumes.

"Don't let them operate on JJ," she said firmly, shifting slightly in her seat.

"Really?"

"Really."

My mind started churning. *We need to go to Seattle.* I had graduated from the University of Washington just months earlier, and immediately got on the phone with everyone I knew there, asking for their recommendations. Every single person I spoke to said the same name: Dr. S.

My mother happened to be undergoing radiation therapy for breast cancer in Seattle just then (further evidence that the Universe has a very dark sense of humor) and she burst into tears when she shared the news with her oncologist that morning. Her doctor, too, recommended Dr. S, and called the Brain Tumor Clinic herself to secure us an appointment with him. We left for Seattle that night.

I was immensely grateful to know that JJ would receive the best possible care. I realized how lucky we were, how privileged. And I confess that I was willing to pull any string I could reach in order to save my husband's life. I'm not proud of that, but it's true.

Surgery was scheduled for about a week after the initial consultation with Dr. S, and in the interim JJ wanted to have a party, "Because I don't know if I'll still be *me* after they take out a chunk of my brain," he said bluntly. "And I want to have one last fun night as *myself.*"

We called it the Fuck the Tumor Party.

· · ·

On the day of surgery, there were so many of us there that we stretched the waiting room's capacity beyond its limits — they finally ended up opening a separate room for us so the other families could have some peace. JJ's parents chatted with mine, while his older sister and her husband entertained their toddler. Friends from out of town arrived, and those who lived nearby flowed in and out. JJ's younger siblings played cards, and we passed the hours reading magazines and drinking cafeteria coffee. I knit him a grey wool hat that ended up way too big, and my beloved friend Meredith held my hand in between rows. Meredith and I found each other in medical school, and ever since then she has always appeared when I needed her. One time, when JJ was at City of Hope and about to undergo another surgery, she found out that I would be waiting alone, in Southern California, during the procedure. She promptly hung up on me, then called me back minutes later to say she was jumping on a plane from Seattle, and would be there at 6:30. She held my hand that day too.

It was a complex procedure lasting almost seven hours, complicated by the tumor's location in his left temporal lobe, near an important language center — the goal was to remove all of the tumor, but if they took too much they risked leaving him speechless. So they proceeded in two phases. First they put him to sleep, and removed the left side of his skull, which was set aside and kept sterile until its presence was again required.

Then they woke him up.

He lay on the operating table, awake and alert, while he was shown a series of flashcards with simple line drawings on them. As the surgeon stimulated the tissue surrounding the tumor with an electrode as fine as a hair, JJ named the images he saw, "Tree. House. Car." When he was unable to name an image or got stuck on one word "Frog-Frog-Frog," they knew they were too close, and backed away until he could find his words again.

The nurse called to give me an update after they finished the mapping and were just about to put him back to sleep so they could do the resection, and in the middle of explaining that everything was going well she said, "I'm sorry, hold on one second." I heard JJ's voice in the background, and paused on the thought that he was speaking from the operating table with half of his skull in a metal tray on the other side of the room, then she came back on the line. "Your husband would like me to tell you not to worry, his sense of humor is intact," she said with a laugh.

Surgeons frequently send small slices of a tumor to the pathologist for review while they're still in the operating room, but Dr. S had warned us that with brain tumors, that initial assessment was notoriously unreliable, "So don't expect any news until I get the formal report," he'd said. "I don't want to send you off on a roller coaster."

But it turned out that the Surgical Resident assisting on the case happened to be a friend. He'd been my resident when I was a medical student doing my surgery rotation, and he couldn't resist sharing the good news when the frozen section came back. He pulled off his surgical mask as he came bounding down the hall, "It looks like it's low-grade!"

It would be weeks before the debating pathologists at the University of Washington and Duke finally came to a consensus. It was ultimately deemed a mixed glioma, predominantly an anaplastic astrocytoma (grade III — which is definitely *not* low-grade).

. . .

Finally, JJ was out of the OR and in the recovery room, groggy but stable. Only immediate family members were allowed in the post-op area, but Brian couldn't bear it, so we told them he was JJ's brother — which was true as far as they were concerned, and the two of us slipped in to see him. JJ was lying on his right side in a faded blue hospital gown with his eyes closed, his head wrapped in miles of gauze, his lower half covered with a sheet and a thin beige blanket. We approached quietly, not wanting to disturb him, and Brian bent down, getting right up to his face, and whispered intently, "Jayge, you doing okay? Just give me a sign brother, some kind of sign to let me know you're in there..."

JJ slowly opened his left eye and motioned Brian around to the other side of the bed. He lifted the thin blanket and sheet and pointed to his bare ass, letting out a little toot. "Sign," he said.

12

FIRST CORRIDOR

"And your husband is...?" The *is* was long and slow. Expectant.

I fought the urge to crush the delicate bones of her limp hand, which I still clasped in an introductory handshake, although handshake may be an inaccurate description, it was more like the offering of a princess — predominantly fingers and slightly raised, awaiting a knight's kiss. She tilted her head just a bit to the right, her brunette curls bouncing, as she awaited my response. I could see her mind working to categorize this new acquaintance, eyebrows slightly arched, porcelain blue doll eyes wide with curiosity. Her words echoed in my mind, ricocheted around bouncing off each other and creating a racket. Somewhere beyond the noise I heard myself say, "Dead."

Her smile froze, and her rosy complexion paled behind the freckles dusting her perky nose. She dropped my hand, unconsciously wiping her own on her sage green capris, presumably to avoid contamination. Taking a quick step back, she turned to the friend who had introduced us, asking frantically, "What? What did she say? Ted? Ned? Fred?"

"No," my friend replied calmly, "she said 'dead.' He died 8 months ago."

It really is a conversation stopper, especially at a fourth-grade open house.

I couldn't help but giggle at the absurdity of it all. I reached out and touched her arm, leaning forward to say, "I'm so sorry, I didn't mean to drop that on you, the question just took me by surprise." But I was speaking into a void, my words dissipating long before they reached her ears.

She was riveted to my friend's face, searching it for some other truth. It was as if I had evaporated. She could no longer see me, or hear my awkward attempts to lighten the mood, albeit with some rather dark humor. Even when I placed my face directly in her line of sight and smiled, "It's OK, you can look at me," her gaze continued on just past my left ear, focused on something far in the distance. I had vanished.

Was she mortified? Terrified? Shocked that tragedy could strike so close to home? Paralyzed by the thought, "If it could happen to them...?" Perhaps she carried her own private pain and I had touched a nerve, or maybe she just thought I was a horribly unkind person to throw it out there so nakedly, and decided she wanted nothing to do with me. I'll probably never know. She has not looked at me since.

Which is understandable, really. It's hard to look suffering in the face, all the more so when that face resembles your own. None of us knows how we will respond when confronted with the unimaginable. Until we are. And then we do.

∽

Halloween marks what we have come to know as The Corridor. Soon after the candy has been gobbled up, the boys birthdays arrive (with one day in between), quickly followed by Thanksgiving and Christmas and New Year's Eve, and then it's January 11. The Anniversary. What we learned that first year is that your body won't let you ignore it. Your body knows the change of seasons, the shortening of the days, the coming of the rain. Even when your mind wants to forget, to block out the endless loop... *this time last year*... your body won't let you. It remembers.

That first trip down The Corridor was bleak. It is long and dim, that passageway, lined with tall narrow doorways, each one opening onto a gaping abyss, deep and dark and terrifying. Each one threatening to suck me in if I veered too close to the edge, and if that happened I feared I'd never escape. The only safe thing to do was focus on the goal: *Just make it through the anniversary.* What I didn't understand that first time, though, was that the only way to bring the sunlight back into The Corridor is to fling open the doors. Look into the abyss. Befriend the monsters that lurk there, and mine their gifts.

∾

We couldn't bear the idea of Christmas at home that first year. The holidays had always been so festive in our house: JJ would strap on his climbing harness and rappel off the chimney to string lights all the way around the roof, and the boys would pick out a tree. Afterwards we would sip hot chocolate with too many marshmallows, pull out the big bins of decorations, and unwrap the angel made by Haitian artisans from oil drums that had washed up on their shores during one in a heartbreaking series of disasters. The

Christmas pyramid from my childhood sat on the dining room table, the heat from its short red candles rising up, pushing the thin wooden fins forward and making the miniature merry-go-round spin. At which point JJ could reliably be heard to say with delight, "See gentlemen, life is physics!"

Every night of December we cursed ourselves for introducing the Elf on the Shelf to our children. The Elf's job was to keep an eye on the kiddos, and duly report both their nice and their naughty behavior back to Santa. This was a task best accomplished from a hidden vantage point of course, to ensure the legitimacy of his report, so each night, once they were sound asleep, he would use his magic to fly around the house seeking the perfect spot from which to spy for the coming day. And the first thing the kids would do when they woke in the morning was hunt for the Elf.

Without fail, hours after we'd gone to bed, "Babe, did you move the Elf?"

Groan. "No, did you?"

"Oh my God, that fucking Elf."

When it was our turn to host the big family feast, JJ would spend days preparing and smoking an enormous roast, determined to outdo my cousin David, who had introduced him to the joys of smokey meat — and promptly challenged him to a running smoke-off when I gave JJ his own Traeger (seriously — best gift ever). We would eat too much and drink too much; it was always loud and raucous and jolly.

I have a photo of our last Christmas together. It's black and white, a little blurred around the edges. We are all gathered around JJ, he is tucked under a blanket on my cousin's sofa. Everyone is smiling. His eyes twinkle, he is enjoying himself even if he can't say so. When I look at

myself, perched behind him with my hand resting on his
shoulder, I catch my breath for a moment. It's physical,
really, a tingly numbness that starts at the top of my head
and slowly follows gravity to my toes, pausing for a while in
the center of my chest. *She has no idea.*

We decided on Maui for our first Christmas as a
tricycle, because that was where we'd gone on our last
family trip, when Culby turned 10 and we told him he
could pick anywhere in the United States for us to have an
adventure. Frankly, Hawaii hadn't occurred to us, but what
could we say when he'd cheerfully pointed out that it was
the 50th state? The boys wanted to go back to Cheeseburger
in Paradise in Lahaina, where we'd spent hours playing
cards and eating fries when the only road back to our hotel
was closed because of an accident; and to a luau, of course.
They wanted to snorkel at Molokini Crater, go whale
watching on a catamaran, and explore the tide pools at
Keawakapu Beach. I drew the line at staying in the same
condo, but we weren't far away.

They were hunting memories. Traces of their father
that they could grasp for a moment, that they could savor
before tucking them away with their treasures. They were
beginning to understand that there would be no new stories,
that those we had were therefore precious and sacred. And
they were avid collectors. Everywhere we went,
"Remember when Dad swam so far away from the boat
cause he was following a sea turtle?"

"Remember when we went on that submarine and Dad
made everyone sing *We all live in a yellow submarine*?"

"Remember when Dad went up on stage at the luau to
learn how to hula dance?"

"Remember when..."

Our Christmas condo was on the ground level, with

sliding glass doors that opened onto a small patio and an expanse of spiky grass that led down to the pool, and the beach beyond. We decorated the miniature tree I'd brought in my suitcase, and set it up in the corner. We strung fairy lights around the room, and draped our stockings over the air conditioner. Then we pulled on our bathing suits and went to the beach.

It was surreal in the way of the Tropics, everything bold and bright, the contrast turned all the way up. But it's vague in my memory. We did all the things; I know, because of the photos. But when I focus on a specific moment it blurs, bleeds into others, and I can't untangle the new from the old; the *before* from the *after*. Like standing in the eye of a hurricane under a deep blue sky, watching all you know blend into one enormous cloud that whirls around you, moving so fast that it's impossible to discern one thing from another.

I remember we spent Christmas Eve at a Holiday Luau, distracted from our grief for a moment by pulled pork and Fire Dancers. I remember Christmas Day was quiet.

∾

One of our favorite couples moved away from Portland in 2013, the same weekend that we moved back there from Spokane, and we had cursed the timing. Our consolation, however, was that it freed up two coveted spots at Lee and Jen's Annual New Year's Eve Feast. They had a very strict rule that they would only invite as many people as could sit comfortably around the table for the multi-course meal, complete with vellum printed menus. The preparations would take days, and Lee outdid himself every year. If you are ever lucky enough to score an invitation to a meal

prepared by Chef Lee, you would be a fool to pass it up. Jen
would cover the table with aluminum foil — shiny side up,
and set it impeccably with all manner of festive party favors
scattered among the assorted china and wine glasses. Lee
worked in the kitchen, giving direction to his helpers, while
we gathered and nibbled on the delicacies spread over the
kitchen table and encroaching on the island. We sipped
cocktails, and made sure everyone had dollar bills for Shut
the Box.

When it was time for dinner we would take our
assigned seats, the Chef would explain the menu, and we
would begin the first course. Often we were still eating at
midnight, but we'd pause for champagne and kisses. We
would write down a favorite memory from the year on small
slips of paper and put them all in a glass bowl, to be read
aloud one by one, while we guessed whose was whose.
After dinner we moved the furniture aside and had a dance
party; everyone's favorite dance partner was Wilson, the
150 pound golden retriever who loved to dance with his
front paws up on your shoulders. We drank too much and
stayed up too late, and had the kind of fun that springs from
shared history and deep friendship.

On JJ's last New Year's Eve, we'd missed the party, but
not the feast. Nor the friendship. Cocktail hour had been at
our house rather than Lee and Jen's, and then a series of
runners had delivered each course to us as it was served up by
Chef Lee. They also brought with them so much love, that I
found myself weeping sporadically. I have a photo of that
night too, it's hard to look at. We are all surrounding JJ,
everyone embracing and smiling. He is lying in the hospital
bed, smiling too, and raising a small green glass of ice cold
tequila with a tiny triangle of lime, aloft, in a toast. When I
look at the photo, I forget how to breathe. The shock is

stunning, because he looks nothing like he did in life. Nothing like the image I carry, like who I see when I close my eyes at night. And I think he would be glad to know that. To know that I remember him as he lived, rather than as he died.

That year was Lee and Jen's last New Year's Eve Feast. We go out for dinner now.

∿

January 11.

The last First.

Just let me get through this day, then I'll be able to stand upright again.

I woke up at exactly 3:00 in the morning, disoriented for a moment. Until I rolled over and reached for him. And when he wasn't there, I sensed the avalanche rumbling. I braced myself for the impact, hunkered down deep inside myself in the crash position. Held my breath. Waited to be crushed. My mind wandered as I lay curled up in the fetal position, watching the clock...

This is when I told him he could go, that we'd be OK.

This is when he took his last breath.

This is when I called Hospice and burst into tears when they asked me what funeral home I would be using.

This is when I sat in the kitchen googling "Funeral Home Near Me."

This is when I broke my children's hearts.

This is when I removed the catheter, dressed him, tried to protect his dignity.

This is when they put him in a long black bag, and zipped it up.

I ran to the bathroom and vomited.

My wedding ring caught the light as I knelt by the toilet, breaking it into all the colors, and splaying them across the pale grey walls, and JJ whispered in my ear, "You can't lose what's real, Doll."

It wasn't my original engagement ring. He had smuggled that one to Mexico clipped to his keys, and slipped it onto my ring finger on a deserted beach, on the last day of the 20th century. Nor was it my original wedding band, the one that had been blessed on our wedding day. No. In a melodramatic bit of foreshadowing, I had lost those rings 18 months before he died.

My five girlfriends and I had taken our eleven kids to the coast for the weekend, and stayed in the perfect house — three full levels, plenty of bathrooms, right near the beach... it was loud and busy and fun.

When I glanced at my hand and realized it was naked, I panicked. We searched every dusty nook and crumby cranny of that rental — unearthing generations of broken barrettes, lego pieces, individual keys, and loose change that all had a sticky film on it for some reason — but no rings. When I finally accepted my fate and called JJ to tell him, I was prepared for him to be quietly furious — he'd been warning me for years that I was going to lose those rings if I kept setting them down in random spots to rub in hand cream or sunscreen.

"J," I burst into tears the second he answered the phone, "I lost my wedding rings!" I was fully sobbing as I leaned on my car hood in the driveway. Dog walkers and sunset strollers heading down to the beach looked at me with varying degrees of concern and bemusement.

"Doll, take a breath, it's okay." But it wasn't okay. Those rings were my talisman. They connected me to him, made him real even when we were apart. Losing them felt ominous, foreboding.

"Sarita, Darling, those rings are just things, just symbols. They *represent* our love, but they're *not* our love. You can't lose what's *real*, Doll."

When the boys and I got home the next day I was still a mess. I called my mom and wept as I told her the story. And as I was hanging up with her, JJ came into the room with a small box, "So, I know it's not your birthday till tomorrow, but I just can't stand to see you so upset," he set the box down in front of me. "Happy Birthday, Doll."

I blew my nose and slowly opened the box. Nestled into the black velvet were three perfect diamonds, one large and two small, "When I got you that first diamond, I was the only man in your life, so a solitaire was right. But now there are three of us, so you should have three."

You can't lose what's real.

Culby and Charlie stayed home from school on that First Anniversary, and we spent the day lounging in our pajamas watching Star Wars movies and eating junk food. We lit the fire, and snuggled up in front of JJ's enormous TV, and in between features we looked at pictures and shared memories. We had moments of gut wrenching pain and fits of hysterical laughter. It was brutal.

Later, after the boys went to bed, I sat alone on the edge of the bathtub, fiddling with my wedding rings. They still encircled my left ring finger, nestled into the groove that had grown deep over the years. A physical imprint of him on my body. In my heart I was still married, and taking them off felt like a betrayal. An acquiescence. It felt so, *final*. Concrete evidence that I was no longer a Wife, but a

Widow, now. I pulled off the two thin bands of tiny diamonds, and put them on my right hand, still in need of a talisman, something tangible, proof of him. I put the ring with the three stones in the small clay bowl Charlie made for me one Mother's Day, with my other treasures.

We made it through The Year of Firsts, I thought, as I lay in bed late that night, tears pooling in my ears, *It'll get better now, right?*

13

KICKING IT FORWARD

(2004)

It was the spring of 2004, and I had been having a recurring dream almost nightly, since JJ's first surgery in February. In it, I am watching from somewhere high above as he wanders, lost in a maze. An overgrown labyrinth, dark and treacherous. I feel his desperation mounting, his fear, as he runs from one dead end to the next, then retraces his steps, trying to distinguish where he took the wrong turn. He is searching for something, I don't know what, but I feel the depth of his despair, the urgency of his quest. I try to call to him, to tell him that he's not alone, that I'm here and I will help him, but my voice doesn't reach him. It's only an echo. And I feel his utter desolation when he cries out into the darkness for help, but cannot make a sound.

I wake up weeping every time.

~

At first, he had only a handful of words at his disposal, so those he could access were in heavy rotation. Flexibility was required. And patience.

"I'll kick it forward and then kick it back," he would say, inevitably surprised when his meaning wasn't obvious.

"I'm sorry Babe, I'm not sure what you're telling me," I would reply, a little piece of my heart breaking off.

Thus began a conversation one day, as we stood in the kitchen, "I'm kicking it *forward*. Then kicking it *back*," he said again, with a note of irritation.

"Okay, are you going somewhere?"

"No."

"Are you going to shower?"

"No."

"Are you thinking of dinner?"

"NO!" The number of volleys he could tolerate was variable, "I AM KICKING IT FORWARD! THEN KICKING IT BACK!" He glared at me before wheeling around and storming out the back door. I watched as he disappeared into the garage, and emerged with the lawn mower. *How long would it have taken me to get to that?*

Later, I picked up the checkbook and noticed that the numbers in the record didn't make sense. Some were transposed, others had been scratched out and rewritten multiple times. The math was off, and I could see where frustration had taken over, the pressure of pen on paper leaving deep grooves. I could picture him in that moment — eyes squinting, brow furrowed, his grip on the pen tightening as he searched his mind in vain. A teardrop landed on the page, pooling in the grooves and blurring the ink.

JJ was used to being the smartest guy in the room, or at least one of them. Accustomed to expressing himself easily and eloquently, with charm and wit, even with a hint of arrogance at times, in the way of those to whom knowledge and learning come easily. So when he found himself trapped alone in his mind, unable to verbalize even the simplest thought, his short-term memory a collection of holes swallowing up the moments of his day, it was his very worst nightmare. His Orwellian rat.

And he couldn't even talk about it.

He found his words slowly, and with great effort. We put labels on doors and sofas and mirrors, like you do when your children are learning to read, and I stopped finishing his sentences. He developed a habit of narrating his life, putting words to the world around him as he went about his day. I frequently found myself asking, "Are you talking *to* me, or just *near* me?" when he would enter a room halfway through a sentence. Eventually, he collected enough words to communicate, but it was years before his speech was fluent, and he never did find them all.

～

"You know this is what's going to kill him, right?" I froze, fork in mid air, and stared across the table at my friend's mother, who happened to be a pathologist, and who rarely filtered her thoughts.

"Well, I'm trying not to think about that right now," I said slowly, around the lump in my throat that signaled the end of lunch for me. The surgery had been successful. JJ was still riding his bike to daily radiation treatments, and he was tolerating the chemotherapy well. The fact that only 30% of people with his type of tumor were still alive at three years was a shadow lurking in the corner, one that I could not bring myself to look at directly, for fear of making it real.

~

It was 2:30 am, five months after JJ's surgery, and I was the senior resident on call in the hospital, charged with overseeing the care of the patients on our service, and responding to any emergencies. When my pager went off, I expected it to be a call from the Emergency Department asking me to come and admit a patient, so I was surprised when Dr. T, one of the Pulmonary/Critical Care attendings, answered the phone and asked me to check on one of his partner's patients.

"Sure, what's her story?"

"It's terrible, really, a 26 year old female with stage IV lung cancer — athlete, never smoked a day in her life, and she has a three-year-old at home — in with pneumonia. She's full code as of now, but if we need to intubate her we may never get her off the vent. The nurse just called me and she's dropping her sats and her work of breathing is going up. I'm not sure what she's on for the pneumonia, you'll have to look at her chart, but it sounds like we need to address goals of care."

Ummm...wait — this is my first rotation as a senior resident. She's never laid eyes on me. She's not on our service. She's crumping, and he's asking me to have this conversation?

"Okay," I said. There wasn't time to discuss it, she was in extremis.

"I really appreciate it, give me a ring after you sort it out."

After I sort it out, right.

She was sitting up at the edge of the bed, the mask of the CPAP machine obscuring everything but her eyes, which were wide with fright and effort. Her chest rose and fell, her neck muscles straining with each breath, and she was covered in a film of sweat beneath the hospital gown that hung off her thin shoulder. The X-ray tech paused to show me the chest x-ray as he wheeled the portable machine away. The respiratory therapist drew a blood gas, the nurse checked her vital signs, and an elegant middle aged woman sat out of the way, in a hard plastic chair pushed back from the bedside.

"Hi Amy, I'm Dr. Bovitz," I said. I sat beside her on the bed and spoke loudly enough for her to hear me over the sound of the machine that was trying to force oxygen into her damaged lungs. "I'm the senior resident here in the hospital tonight, and Dr. C's partner asked me to come and see you."

The woman in the chair leaned forward, her brow furrowed and her lips pursed with worry, "Well, where is he? When is he coming?" Amy waved her hand feebly, focused solely on her struggle to breathe.

"Dr. T is covering for him tonight, but he's at home and since I'm here already he asked me to come and assess her." I reached out my hand to shake hers, "You must be a family member?"

"I'm her mother," she said, tears pooling in her tired eyes. "Her husband's at home with their son, we're taking turns..."

It was clear that if we were going to be aggressive and try to get her through the pneumonia she would need to be intubated. But it was also clear that Dr. T was right — her cancer was advanced, and if we put her on the ventilator, she might never come off, meaning she would never be able to say goodbye to her husband and young son, and the last days or weeks of her life would be spent sedated, with a machine breathing for her. And then her family would face the additional pain of withdrawing care. But she was so young... I leaned forward and placed my hand on her mother's knee.

"I'm so sorry that I'm the one having this conversation with you. I know we've never met before and it's hard to trust a stranger, but we have to make a decision and either intubate her, or change our focus to keeping her comfortable. She's not able to tell me what she wants right now because she's working so hard to breathe, so I need you to help me do what she would tell me to do if she could." She looked at me blankly as I continued, "I know how painful this is..."

Her expression hardened, and she may as well have spoken the words out loud:

You have no idea how painful this is.

It was as if a physical wall had slammed down between us, her gaze shifted to the peonies on the small table just past my shoulder. And I wasn't sure how much she was taking in as I explained the options.

"I really do know how hard this is... on a personal level," I said, placing my hand on hers. "I promise I'm not speaking in platitudes."

Her face softened slightly and a tear slid down to the corner of her mouth, "It's just so hard..."

Several hours later Amy was stabilized and sedated, on the ventilator in the ICU. I sipped a tepid cup of coffee as I worked on my notes in the small cubby outside her room. The glass door slid open, and her mother emerged.

"Doctor," she said quietly, "I have to ask you something."

"Of course," I swiveled around on the tall backless stool where we always perched to do paperwork. "How can I help you?"

"Earlier, upstairs," she said swallowing, bracing herself, "you alluded to something — you said you really do know how hard this is..." She looked at me pleadingly, and my heart ached for her. She needed to know that she was not alone in her pain, she needed evidence that it was possible to survive it. "Please, I need to know what you meant."

"Well," I said, taking a deep breath, "I've never shared this with a patient before, but my husband is battling cancer too right now."

Her face was aghast. "Oh my goodness I'm so sorry, can I ask what kind?"

"It's a brain tumor. He had surgery and radiation and he's still doing chemo. It's not a great prognosis, so we're just trying to take it one day at a time."

We were both weeping now, and I stood up and stepped closer. "Would it be OK if I gave you a hug?" I asked.

We held each other for a moment, finding comfort in our mutual suffering and the release that comes from sharing your pain with another soul who *gets it*.

"I'm just so very sorry," I said softly.

She leaned back, gripping my arms and struggling to keep her voice steady as she said, "Oh sweetheart, these tears aren't for me... they're for you."

It can be complicated, doctoring while human.

In medical school we are taught to maintain appropriate boundaries, to empathize without commiserating, to listen to our patients' stories, not share our own. What I learned that night was that sometimes healing goes beyond the medical treatments. Sometimes the human part just matters more.

· · ·

JJ was still sleeping when I got home in the morning, always on his right side now, the left side still tender.

"Babe," I whispered in his ear, "good morning. I have to tell you about last night."

He smiled before opening his eyes, and reached out to pull me toward him.

"Good morning, Doll," he said, wrapping his arms around me as I snuggled into his chest. "So, tell me about your night."

"Well, there was this patient..." He held me tighter as the story tumbled out, "and J, ever since I shared your story with her I can't stop worrying that I violated your privacy somehow. I mean it's yours to tell, not mine, and I'm so sorry if you're not okay with that, and I just needed to tell you..."

He was quiet for a moment, slowly identifying the words he needed and painstakingly putting them together in the appropriate order, and then he said, "First off, it's not *my* story — it's *our* story. And it sounds like she really needed that, I'm glad you had *our* story to tell her. Some good's gotta come out of this, right?"

14

SECOND SPRING

A bit of magical thinking, to be sure, but when I woke up on January 12, 2018, I expected to feel different somehow. I had done it after all, I had survived every excruciating minute of The Year of Firsts. I had mastered the PB&J, for God's sake. But the fog was still there, still thick around me, still obscuring anything beyond the immediate. It was impossible to imagine the future — it brought me to my knees every time I tried.

It was a dark time, lonely, no matter who was nearby. And my greatest fear was getting stuck there, becoming mired in it.

What is wrong with me? Shouldn't I be feeling better? Why can't I just snap out of it...?

∾

It was the children being ripped from their parents' arms and locked up in cages at the Mexican border that caused something to shift inside me. Prompted me to look up for a

minute, reminded me of the world outside of our grief.
That, and the elephants.

JJ's little sister Kate and her husband Vijay were
married for the first time that spring, in Vijay's hometown
Chennai, which lies on the Southeastern coast of India on
the Bay of Bengal. It was to be the first joyous family
celebration without JJ, and the first big trip the boys and I
would take as a tricycle. I was exuberant and terrified in
equal measure. Charlie had turned ten that fall, so it was his
turn to choose a family adventure, and since we would
already be in India, we decided to go on to Thailand, where
we would spend three days at an elephant sanctuary.

I got to work on the many arrangements to be made — the
visa applications and updated passports, the immunizations
and just-in-case medications, the multiple flights and hotels
and the transportation in-between, it was a lot to keep track of
and required many, many lists. And it was a struggle, because
grief is profoundly disorganizing. It unwires you, leaves your
mind frayed and your body worn, so that even the most
ordinary task requires a summoning of all your forces. Those
more complex require a focus that can be elusive.

When booking our flights I neglected to take the
International Date Line into account and reserved a hotel in
Singapore for an overnight layover that didn't exist. I'd
made sure the boys' passports were valid, but hadn't noticed
that they would expire while we were in Thailand. And it
wasn't until the very last minute that I remembered to
arrange a house sitter to take care of our pets. Even so, with
each completed task, I felt a sense of accomplishment —
pride even. It felt good to harness my mind for a minute.

Chennai was a whirlwind. Beautiful and emotional and
complicated. Harder than I'd imagined. My memories are

fractured. Frozen bits that hang in-between long moments filled with JJ's absence. Exploring ancient ruins and visiting sacred temples. Riding camels and lunches served on banana leaves. Beautiful Kate on her wedding day, her hands and feet decorated with intricate henna designs, fresh blooms in her hair. The warmth and grace of two families merging into one. Beginnings, and endings.

Then we were in Thailand, and I had planned all of our adventures with JJ whispering in my ear. So we ziplined through the jungle canopy and rafted the Mae Taeng River. We took a cooking class, learned to make fresh curry paste and authentic Khao Soi. We explored Buddhist temples and wandered among the stalls of the nighttime markets. We trekked along a stream to a stunning waterfall tucked deep in the jungle, past sacred trees identified by Buddhist monks with orange strips of cloth tied around their boughs. We spent a few days on a stunning beach, so perfect it felt like a movie set, where the boys learned Thai boxing techniques from the hotel manager and drank mocktails at sunset. It was all amazing to be sure, but nothing could compare to the elephants.

We arrived at the sanctuary in time to help serve breakfast. After reviewing basic machete safety (especially important for 10 and 12 year old boys who love nothing more than a good sword fight) we got straight to work chopping mountains of sugar cane into elephant-sized bites, which we then offered, by way of an introduction, to the giants with their soulful eyes. They wandered around an open pasture in the misty early morning light, each elephant accompanied by a personal Mahout, a caregiver and trusted companion who spent 24 hours a day by their side. Their bond was so deep that the veterinarian would not even begin an exam unless the Mahout was present to provide comfort and reassurance.

These elephants had been rescued from lives of hard labor and abuse, our host Chet explained, and were treated with compassion and respect. "We consider this the second best life for an elephant. The best life for an elephant is to be free, living in the forest, but these creatures have never been free, so they don't know how to survive on their own." Before his death in 2016, Chet told us, King Bhumibol had tried to re-introduce rescued elephants to the wild, "But they just stood around, waiting for someone to feed them. They didn't know what to do."

I was drawn to an ancient blind female who stood completely still with her trunk raised and her diamond shaped mouth wide open, waiting patiently for her breakfast. "She was rescued from an illegal logging operation," Chet said. "They would have killed her because she can't work enough to pay for her keep, but one of the workers tipped us off, and we convinced them to let us bring her here." I pulled a chunk of sugar cane from the bag slung over my shoulder and tentatively placed it on her tongue, pink and strong and wet. She closed her mouth before I could withdraw my hand, which was vaguely terrifying, but she did not start chewing until I had pulled it out — a sensation I imagine as similar to exiting the vaginal canal.

We were each paired with an elephant for the duration of our stay, and my partner was named Isra, which means freedom. She had belonged to a family, their most valuable possession, and spent most of her life in chains. This was not because her owners were bad people, Chet explained, "They just didn't know any better." We learned to watch their body language — a swishing tail for example was a relaxed sign, whereas a rigid tail meant they were anxious. We learned that flapping their ears was just a cooling mechanism, but stiff outstretched ears meant they were trying to look intimidating. And that the low rumbling sounds they made were just conversations, but a trumpet was a warning. We learned too, that these magnificent creatures live rich and complex emotional lives, they experience joy and love and grief and rage. Just like we do. You could see it in their eyes.

Culby loved the picnic in the forest, when the Mahouts split a piece of bamboo and balanced it between two thin forked branches placed over a small fire to cook scrambled eggs, while the elephants grazed around us. Charlie's favorite thing was the baths. Twice a day, we would lead the elephants to a pond with a gently sloping shore, and their pace would quicken as we approached — they loved it too. The Mahouts would hand us buckets and stiff scrub brushes, and we dodged fountains of water as the giants frolicked while we scrubbed their backs and behind their ears. It's quite an intimate thing, bathing an elephant.

∼

We arrived home to the New York Times headline: "Hundreds of Immigrant Children Have Been Taken From Parents at U.S. Border".

What?

Then it was the images of families reaching for each other as they were dragged apart, their faces awash with tears of fear and fury and desperation. It was the inconsolable toddlers who would be forever scarred, that early trauma seared onto their cells like plastic melted over an open flame. It was the immeasurable pain of a mother, her shirt soaked with breast milk, her baby lost to her.

I hadn't been in the habit of following the news for quite some time, to be honest, but this sliced right through the haze, my outrage instant and hot. It forced me to peek out from beneath my grief, to acknowledge that the rest of the world had indeed continued on, even as we hovered in the void. It reminded me, as the elephants had, that we were not the only souls that suffered; and for a moment, my heart felt strong enough to carry it. The thing was, I simply had no reserve. I was quickly depleted, overwhelmed by all of the chaos and callousness, and I reflexively folded in on myself once again. But not quite as deeply, I noticed.

It was a start.

15

THE RED THREAD

(2005-2007)

It was a complicated time. Labile. Especially so in the beginning, before we could bring ourselves to accept one simple fact: This was our story now. Before we could begin to understand that now it was up to us, to choose who we would become in light of it. We were elated after each negative MRI, but then our exaltation would slowly fade, replaced by a creeping sense of dread as the next one approached. The night before every follow-up appointment with the oncologist, we would go out for a nice dinner — just in case. It was an exercise in elasticity.

And patience. And forgiveness. Because circumstance was forcing our hand, requiring us to face the very best and the very worst in ourselves. And frankly, it wasn't always easy to look at. There were times when I failed him. When I couldn't see past myself, when I was selfish and thoughtless. Times when I expected him to be *him*, even though I knew that wasn't fair, times when I allowed myself to become angry about it all. And there were times when his anger too, boiled over and he lashed out at me, because I was the stand-in for the enemy he couldn't reach. I was the safe place to put it all. But even on those darkest days, we forgave each other quickly and without reserve — and we were grateful that we never seemed to be at our very worst at the same time. That we could balance each other out.

~

There is a Chinese proverb that says:

An invisible red thread connects those who are destined to meet. Regardless of time, place, or circumstance. The thread may stretch or tangle, but it will never break.

It's such a lovely image. And so very complicated.

I was finally in my last year of residency, and JJ was proving to be an outlier — there was no evidence of residual tumor on the MRIs he had every three months, and the statistical likelihood of his survival was increasing each day, confirming what we knew in our hearts to be true. We were confident that he would beat the odds — in our minds, there was simply no other option. And he was determined to continue moving forward with our life because, "Otherwise, what a waste of time, Doll!" So we carried on — he with his graduate work and me with my training, us with our life.

And eventually, we dared to look up. One day, we even caught ourselves dreaming of the future again. Of the family we would make, of the adventures we would have, of the work we would do. It felt indulgent at first, decadent. And fraught. But the earth beneath our feet had begun to solidify. A path forward was slowly emerging — we could see it through the haze if we squinted. Would we be brave enough to choose it? Or would we shrink into ourselves, and live out our days paralyzed by the unknowable?

What if the tumor comes back?

What if it doesn't?

What if our life is cut short?

What if it isn't?

What if we...?

What if we don't...?

Then we felt the tug of the Red Thread.

"That's him!" JJ's face lit up as he pointed across the cavernous lobby of The Westin Camino Real hotel in Guatemala City, where dozens of women, each holding a small bundle, gathered under the two story domed ceiling with gilded trim, a multi-tiered chandelier dangling from the center. A colossal bouquet of exotic flowers, so perfect that you assumed they were fake until you drew close enough to catch a perfumed whiff, stood centered on an elaborately carved wooden table that echoed the round shape of the room, and small collections of mostly white couples like us sat around granite topped coffee tables in high backed chairs decorated with gold leaf. The juxtaposition of privilege and struggle was breathtaking.

"That's our son! Right there!" JJ declared. But that was just silly — they were much too far away, and it was entirely too crowded to see clearly. But he was right. Araceli, our local adoption coordinator, smiled quietly as she rose and made her way over to the group of women, embracing the one holding a baby boy wrapped in a blue blanket covered with stars, and leading her back across the room toward us.

As they crossed the marble inlayed floor, past the grand piano and the mural depicting a version of Indigenous life that was utterly inconsistent with any known reality, we felt the Red Thread grow taut.

JJ and I had always planned to adopt, we talked about it at great length before we got married. Neither of us felt any particular biologically-driven urge to pass on our genes to the next generation. We figured with six and a half billion people already at that time, the pool was big enough. We knew that love does not require shared DNA, and we both felt drawn to the many children at risk of growing up without a Forever Family. It seemed obvious to us both, and I suppose that was the very first tug of the Red Thread. We decided that if we did happen to get pregnant — well, that would be a great experience for *us,* one that we would embrace and celebrate, but we both saw pregnancy vs parenting as rather like a wedding vs a marriage: joyous and profound and deeply meaningful, but really just an overture to the opus.

"Our children will find us," JJ had said, on more than one occasion. "It doesn't matter whether they come through us, or to us."

When we felt the pull of the Red Thread, first with Culby and then two years later with Charlie, we followed it, without question or doubt. Because we knew that it led to our children, that we were already connected, that we were destined to meet.

But we also understood that our joy was born of suffering. That the mothers who sacrificed of themselves, who created and nurtured and birthed these singular human beings, and then entrusted them to us to cherish as they did, did so out of necessity — not choice. That a lifetime of war and poverty and struggle had robbed them of their freedom. We understood that our destinies were all intertwined. That the Red Threads connecting each of us may stretch and tangle, yes, but they will never break.

16

SECOND SUMMER

L ong after the communal tears have dried and life has resumed its rhythm, you find yourself alone with your grief. It's your closest companion, an ever-present shadow that weighs a thousand tons. Sometimes you collapse beneath its mass, knees buckling, hands shaking, body fluids everywhere. And sometimes it sits quietly beside you, one tendril coiled loosely around your heart, lulling you into a false sense of safety before it blindsides you. It's constant. And brutal.

And yet, the prospect of leaving it behind is terrifying.

Grieving is our final act of love, after all. Our last connection. Our pain stands as the only remaining evidence of all that we lost. How do you turn away from that? To separate yourself from your grief requires an untangling of the fibers that wove your lives together, but then you're left with a tangle of random threads that make no sense alone. *Where is the tapestry that was our life? And what the hell do I do with all these threads?*

It's that process of weaving a life back together that is so daunting. And lonely, because people have expectations. I saw a survey that asked how long people thought it took to grieve the death of a loved one. On average, the answer was six months. Well, I find that hilarious.

Sometimes, your loved ones see what they need to see. They need you to be okay, so they don't notice the fine cracks in your veneer. And you don't point them out, because who wants to be *That Person*. The one who is truly and deeply broken. Who struggles with small talk. Who is lost, and unsure who she will be on the other side. Who doesn't know how to ask for help because she doesn't even know what she needs. Whose world is at once collapsing in on itself and exploding so violently that the residue of that former life is being flung to the farthest reaches of her soul. What a bore!

But something was stirring in me. Becoming restless. Curious, even.

Who am I now?

At first, the very thought paralyzed me. Sent me deep into the safety of my suffering. An unanswerable question, best left unasked.

Then, my mind could actually hold it for a moment. Only for a moment at first, but that was something.

And eventually, I found myself looking straight at it — turning it over, testing its reflection in the light. Marveling at the kaleidoscope.

Not that I had any idea what the answer was.

～

"I can't wait to visit Daddy's tree!" Charlie squealed. "That's the first thing I'm gonna do when we get to Cape Lookout!" It was Fourth of July weekend and I was loading the camping gear into the car, sweating profusely and wondering why it never occurred to me to wait and shower after the car was packed. I was slowly getting this camping thing down, though, developing my own system. When it had finally occurred to me that I could do that — that I didn't have to agonize over recreating JJ's very specific and elaborate version, that it was okay to eat hot dogs and cereal, that we really didn't need three of everything — it became so much easier.

"Okay guys — wheels up!" We piled into the car with happy hearts, looking forward to a weekend of friendship and fun, some time with our people, in our sacred spot. The weather turned as we drove toward the coast, clouds rolling in and the temperature dropping, and for a moment I worried it might dampen the delight.

But the boys didn't care, "We're Portland kids, Mom!" they proclaimed proudly. "You don't let a little rain stop you if you're from Portland — you'd never do anything!"

I hopped out of the car to check us in at the ranger station, and as the ranger was filling out our parking pass, he said, "So you just go down toward the water, and follow the road around to the right. The group sites are all the way down."

I looked at him blankly, "Wait, did you say to the right?" He nodded. "But, the group sites are to the left," I said slowly, wondering if he was new.

"Not anymore," he said with an apologetic look. "The erosion was so bad this year the whole bluff was washed away, and we just don't have the resources to maintain it."

"Wait, what?" I must have misunderstood him.

"Yeah, so that whole area's closed, and the group sites are over on the other side now, with the rest of the campground." I stood there, staring at him stupidly, unable to wrap my mind around what it was that he was saying.

We drove slowly toward the water, the road that goes to the left now blocked by an iron gate. The grass grew tall. The parking area was littered with sharp rocks and tree limbs. The bluff was half naked, the sandbags that had propped it up now revealed for all to see, as it slid down to merge with the beach. It felt forsaken. Lonely. Desolate. The boys faces were grief-stricken. "I'm sure Daddy's tree is still there guys," I said quietly. "We'll unload our stuff and walk over there to see him."

We were silent as we turned down the road that goes to the right, behind a tall dune that stretched the length of the campground, blocking any view of the sea, although we could hear the waves crashing onto the shore, so we knew it was still there. Several large rectangles, demarcated by waist-high chain link fencing, were spaced along the backside of the dune, and signs posted every few feet warned against traversing the dune to reach the shore. It started to drizzle.

With every arrival the conversation began anew:

"Whaaat?!"

"This is awful — it feels like a dog run!"

"We have to walk like a half mile to get over to the beach!"

"There's no place to hang a hammock!"

"We can't even see the ocean!"

"It's the end of an era..."

"What will we do for Labor Day?"

We were all heartbroken. Someone handed me a Pacifico. Someone else turned on The Avett Brothers. Tents went up, dogs and children explored, we made our way down to the beach. Someone handed me another Pacifico. We slowly started to smile, and then eventually to laugh.

Except for Charlie. He was crushed.

"Mom," he said, as we picked our way through the forest, toward the massive cedar with the elegant limbs, "I feel so bad." His eyes filled with tears, "Now we won't come back and visit Daddy any more." He broke down, sobbing in my arms as we stood there in the embrace of JJ's tree, surrounded by ghosts.

A little while later Charlie tugged on my fleece, "Mom," he said with a quiver in his voice, "I want to go home."

"You do sweetheart?" I said, setting down my Pacifico and wrapping my arms around him.

"Yes. It's just too sad, and I want to go home." Tears streamed down his cheeks, and then mine.

"Well my love, I've had a couple of beers so I can't drive us home tonight, but if you really want to leave we can go in the morning," I said, kissing the top of his head.

"Okay," he said. He took a deep breath, steeling himself, and then ran off to play with the other kiddos.

I was sure Charlie would feel better once the shock wore off a little bit. But when he crawled into my sleeping bag the next morning, cheeks still flushed with sleep, hair sticking straight up on one side, warm and snuggly and small, the first thing he said was "When are we leaving?"

He didn't even want to stop at JJ's tree on the way out.

~

After Kate and Vijay's second wedding that summer in Portland, Culby and Charlie flew back to the Midwest with their grandparents to spend some time with their cousins. It was the first time the three of us had been apart since JJ died, and it felt a bit wobbly, suddenly balancing on a unicycle. I threw myself into redecorating their bedrooms, per their very specific instructions, and found myself listening to quite a bit of NPR. Ever since JJ had died, I couldn't stand silence — it left me alone with my thoughts and who knew where that might lead, so in every room, either the radio or the TV played constantly. I never absorbed anything, it was just comforting, the low hum of human voices in the background, white noise holding the dark noise in my head at bay.

But as I struggled to hang a six-by-ten foot reproduction of a vintage Spider Man comicstrip on the angled wall of Culby's bedroom, and an enormous baby elephant that looked like it had five limbs but was really just anatomically correct on Charlie's, some of the background noise crystallized and began to pry its way into the foreground.

I found myself unable to tolerate the belligerence of our 45th president, his voice caused my eyes to glaze over and my mind to attach itself to something else. He struck me as a petulant schoolyard bully, stomping his way across the playground, fawning over tyrants and betraying friends, stealing lunch money and breaking toys for the sheer joy of it. Because he could. It was difficult to take him seriously, because his behavior was just so *childish*.

When I learned that at the G-7 summit in Quebec, he had berated other world leaders over trade policies, left the summit early, and then tweeted from Airforce One that he would not be signing a communique he had agreed to before leaving; that at the NATO summit, he had accused Angela Merkel of being "totally controlled" and "captive to Russia", before holding a joint press conference with Vladimir Putin, in which he disputed the assessment of the US intelligence community that Russia had indeed interfered in the 2016 election; and that he had met with Kim Jong-un for five hours in Singapore, where they had apparently fallen in love, all I could think was, *Oh no, here comes puberty.*

It sounds flippant, I know, but frankly at the time, I had not yet grasped the very real danger he posed — in my mind he was still just a cartoon character.

That was the summer that women drove in Saudi Arabia for the first time. That a liquid lake was discovered on Mars. That fires raged around the world, and Europe battled a measles outbreak. It was the summer that twelve soccer players and their coach were rescued from a flooded underground cave in northern Thailand, and a nineteen-year-old Indonesian boy was found after forty-nine days at sea, adrift atop his fish trap which had become untethered.

It was also the summer that hundreds and hundreds of children remained lost to their parents, frightened and alone, despite a court order to reunite families that had been separated at the border. Because it turned out, nobody had bothered to keep track of them. That's what stayed with me. It was their faces, I saw my own children in them.

∼

"Mom!" Culby yelled, bursting through the front door, "Mom! Guess what!"

"What?" I yelled back from the kitchen where I was washing dishes while Charlie peeled a mountain of miniature oranges.

"My friend Dean's going to live in Spain! For a whole year!" He was still shouting even though he had arrived in the kitchen now, which made us all laugh.

"I know!" I said, drying my hands as I turned to face him "The whole family's going — what do you think about that?"

"I'm so jealous!" he said with a grin.

"Me too!" said Charlie, around a mouthful of mandarin slices.

That gave me pause, "Would you guys be interested in going to live somewhere else for a little while?" I asked. It was an idea that had passed through me right after JJ died, one that I had quickly dismissed because it wasn't like the first time around, when it was just the two of us, and JJ had said "Doll, if I die you're going to Africa, aren't you?" I had two children now, I couldn't just pluck them from the comfort of their home and school and community and plunk them down in a foreign land.

But they hollered simultaneously, "YES!"

"Well, do you think it might be hard, too? I mean Dean's going to be away from his friends, and his school, and his soccer team, and in a place where they speak a different language," I gasped, "What if there's no wifi?"

They were both quiet for a minute, contemplating. Then Culby said solemnly, "Yes, it would be hard. But Mom, it would be so *worth* it!"

Something unfurled a little bit inside me then, loosened slightly.

We sat around the kitchen table all afternoon, eating oranges and discussing the pros and cons of living abroad. The conversation came around to what it would be like to go somewhere less wealthy than Spain, like Guatemala, if I were working with an NGO for example. They both loved the idea, and when Charlie said earnestly, "Yeah — and me and Culby could help the kids there, too!" I felt the fog start to thin. Just a smidge, but enough that I could begin to imagine a blue sky beyond it.

I hadn't returned to work as a hospitalist, it had quickly become apparent that the long hours and complicated schedule were just not compatible with being an only parent. Also, my emotions hovered so close to the surface during those days that I was afraid I might over-empathize to the point of dysfunction, a flood of tears to accompany a diagnosis of diabetes would certainly be awkward. For the last eighteen months I had been focused solely on my children, on the struggle to right our ship, clinging desperately to the hope that I would eventually sort out how to steer it. And slowly but surely, we were figuring it out, we were finding our way.

And I was so grateful for this gift of *time*. So very lucky that JJ had insisted on getting life insurance when we bought our first house, that we had been able to put away some savings, that our family was so incredibly supportive and generous. It had been eighteen months of stopping to repair the wonky wheels of our tricycle, of learning how to grease an axle, replace a bent spoke, repair a broken chain. Of figuring out the physics of life on three wheels.

But, now what?

～

The boys' enthusiasm for adventure was inspiring, and it brought me full circle — brought me right back to Guatemala all those years ago, to bumping up that mountain trail on the back of a motorcycle, to thinking, *If I were a doctor, I could just do it myself...*

Perhaps then, this was my purpose. I could go back to school to study Global Health, and then the boys and I could build the health and education center JJ and I had dreamed of, and split our time between Portland and Guatemala. We could do it. After all, magic happened there.

17

THE PUZZLE

(2005-2007)

"The air! The air!" a petite woman with long black hair tied in a plait that fell to her waist called out as she rushed to our side and covered Culby's face with a cloth. "You must protect the baby from the wind and the dust," she scolded in rapid Spanish, "or he'll catch a cold!" She patted my arm and tilted her head to the side, looking me in the eye for a long moment, not unkindly, but as if she were summing me up, before she turned and disappeared around the corner of the massive Camino Real hotel.

"Is it that obvious that we don't know what we're doing?" JJ asked, turning to me with a grin. "Even random strangers are giving us advice." Just then our taxi arrived, and we double checked that we had the oversized envelope containing all of the official paperwork required to take Culby with us to my old home, Antigua, for the week. And the diapers. And the bottles. And the formula. And the squeezy bulb in case his nose got stuffy. And the cream in case he got diaper rash. And the Tylenol in case he got a fever. And the burp cloths, and the changing mat, and the soft toys, and...

We had been preparing for this moment for close to a year. There had been the applications and the FBI background checks and the letters of reference regarding our character, our finances, our health. The Home Study was nerve wracking, an in-depth examination of our life with all its warts and daisies. Was our house appropriate for children? Were we?

Once we had been approved, we breathed a sigh of relief, and then leapt to answer the phone every time it rang — was this the call? And when it finally was, we wept and laughed and danced. But it would be months still, until we could bring him home. In the meantime he was safe, nurtured and adored by his foster family, who sent us a raft of photos every couple of days — sleeping in his bassinet, wearing the little outfits we sent, snuggling with the big stuffed bear that JJ's mother had given us at the start of our journey — we'd slept with it between us for weeks so that it would absorb some of our smell, and then sent it down when he was born, hoping that when at last we held him in our arms, there would at least be something familiar in our scent.

And we were allowed to visit, as the paperwork moved through the various layers of bureaucracy. While we waited for the final appointment, the one at the embassy in Guatemala City. The one where he would officially become our child on paper, as he already was in our hearts.

At the end of the week, we would have to give him back to his loving foster family, until the adoption was finalized. It would be excruciating. But we weren't ready to think about that yet, all we cared about just then, was bonding with our infant son — he was twelve weeks old already, we had a lot of catching up to do. So we bundled ourselves into the back of the cab, and in the process we broke a Cardinal Rule well known to every parent everywhere: Never Wake a Sleeping Baby.

His cries echoed around the car, bouncing off the windshield and careening back to smack us in the face. Over, and over, and over again. Nothing we did could soothe him, and we tried everything — his diaper was dry, he didn't want a bottle or need to burp, it wasn't too hot or too cold, and he was vehemently disinterested in the brightly colored cloth butterfly with the crinkly wings. The driver's expression remained inscrutable, but I saw his grip on the steering wheel tighten, and at one point I'm pretty sure I heard him whispering a prayer for patience. I fought a growing sense of desperation, my stomach was curling into knots as doubts about my parenting skills forced their way into the foreground. JJ, however, remained unflappable — for which I was both grateful and annoyed.

When we were about ten minutes from our destination, suddenly, and for no apparent reason, Culby opened his eyes wide to JJ's smiling face hovering above him. He looked directly into JJ's eyes, sucked in a deep shuddering breath, and fell silent. It was as if they recognized each other in that moment, realized who it was there, at the other end of that Red Thread. Culby took a bottle then, and promptly fell asleep.

Three of my favorite photos from that week:

JJ and Culby sound asleep in an orange and red striped hammock, swaying in the shade of a weathered wooden pergola swathed in fuchsia bougainvillea, wearing little but matching expressions of pure contentment.

JJ sitting crosslegged on the bed as he changes Culby's diaper, with a baby blanket tied around his nose and mouth like an outlaw from the Wild West. The poor guy was stricken with the dry heaves whenever he encountered bodily waste, and was forced to take extreme defensive measures.

Culby dozing on my chest. If you look closely, you can see his right hand resting on my shoulder, with his middle finger extended. "Well, Doll," JJ had laughed, "we may be in trouble."

"That was the hardest thing I've ever done," I said through my tears as we watched Culby drive off with his foster family at the end of the week. He had cried when we gave him back to his adoring foster parents and their two charming children, whose faces lit up with joy when they saw him. It was both reassuring and heartbreaking.

"I know Doll, but they will love him and nurture him and take good care of him until we can bring him home," he put his arms around me. "It won't be long now..."

We hadn't even finished unpacking when the phone rang, and JJ answered it. I wasn't paying attention, I was in our room, folding laundry and daydreaming about long walks in the park and bath time and bedtime stories...

"Doll!" JJ called as he bounded up the stairs, "It's time! We have our last appointment at the embassy — it's scheduled for the day after tomorrow!" He burst through the door carrying a bottle of champagne, and scooped me up in his arms, spinning me around like it was our wedding day. We sat on the floor in the room that would be Culby's, sipping the champagne and admiring the jungle scene JJ's mother had painted on the walls. The rest of the family had helped with the project too, resulting in a space infused with so much love that you felt it brush your cheek as you entered. JJ was the second of four siblings, and the oldest son. He grew up in a home that was busy and loud and joyful, in a community that was grounded in faith and service and love. Those were his seeds.

There was a lion with a bright orange mane keeping watch next to the changing table, and a red toucan with blue feathers flying above. A giraffe sheltered under a tall tree in one corner, and a smiling monkey swung from a branch in front of a full moon in another. Next to the crib, an elephant drank from a small pond, oblivious to the group of bees closing in on its rump — JJ had painted the lead bee, who pointed toward the elephant with an impertinent grin. There were other tiny creatures scattered around too — a fish peeking up out of the water, a spider dangling from a tall blade of grass, a ladybug perched on the elephant's ear, a bright green caterpillar inching its way along the baseboard. And JJ's mother had recreated all these hidden gems on an oversized light switch plate, which would become Culby's first version of The Matching Game.

It was time.

We could only swing one last minute ticket to Guatemala, so I hopped on the next plane alone, my bag stuffed with baby supplies and gifts for Culby's foster family, a delirious smile plastered across my face. And the next morning, we all wept as Culby's foster family said their goodbyes. They had all come to see him off, and they had each written him a letter. The kiddos had drawn a picture of their neighborhood too, labeling their house, the church, the neighbor's dog. "I hope he remembers us," eight-year-old Lico said.

A friend picked us up and brought us to her house in Antigua, and later that night, I sat on her bed, Culby lying on his back in front of me as I changed his diaper. It was the first time I had been truly alone with him, the first time I was solely responsible for him, and the significance of that fact was soaking into my cells. A brand new sensation melted over me, burgeoning Mother Love was reshaping my heart, expanding it, fusing it irrevocably to this tiny soul. I leaned forward, utterly entranced, "Hi," I said, offering my finger which he grabbed with surprising force, "I'm your mom. I love you more than anything in the world. Forever. And no matter what."

He let out a little toot, startling himself, and the expression on his face was priceless — somewhere between completely confused and deeply satisfied. I burst out laughing, tilting my head back as I tend to do, and with impeccable timing, a golden stream of pee arced through the air and landed directly in my mouth.

Welcome to parenthood.

"I'll wait until everyone else is off, if that's okay," I said to the kind-hearted flight attendant when she asked if I needed a hand, "I just need a minute to pull it together." It had been a surprisingly easy flight to Houston. I'd remembered to give Culby a bottle during takeoff and another during landing, which helped keep his ears from plugging up, and he slept peacefully in-between. Surrounding passengers had commented repeatedly on what a "good baby" he was, which struck me as odd, *Would they have deemed him a "bad baby" if he'd been fussy?* I scanned the area, retrieving the butterfly with the crinkly wings from under my seat, and the empty bottle that had rolled out of sight during our descent. I double checked the oversized manilla envelope that held all of the paperwork we would need for Culby's first entry into the United States, and made sure our passports were easily accessible.

Then I lay Culby down on the center seat, collected the diaper bag, my carryon bag, my purse, and the envelope, setting them all on the aisle seat, and pulled the baby carrier over my head, "Are you ready sweetheart?" I leaned down and gave him a kiss, and a zurbert on his belly which made him giggle. "Okay, let's go!" I moved into the center aisle, and bent down to pick him up, making those silly sound effects that you only use with babies and small animals as I swung him up over my head to slide him into the carrier on my chest —

WHAM!

All the singsongy words lodged in my throat like a string of fish hooks, *Oh my God!* I had not noticed the television monitor hanging from the ceiling above us, and slammed Culby's head right into it when I lifted him up. It was quiet for a long moment, while I pulled him close to my chest and frantically checked for injuries. And then, he let out a wail so loud that I was sure it had to be amplified by the shape of the airplane because that many decibels could not possibly emanate from those two tiny lungs, (it was my first encounter with the truth that the longer the pause, the louder the cry).

My first thought was:

Oh my God, they're going to know that I don't know what I'm doing, and take him away!

My second thought was:

Oh my God, I don't know what I'm doing!

. . .

Culby has always been a great sleeper, ever since that first
nap in the car on the way to Antigua. When he rubbed his
eyes it was a signal that he was ready, and when we lay him
down he would stretch and sigh contentedly, and be fast
asleep within minutes. I, on the other hand, was obsessed
with the baby monitor, and would spring up, wide eyed and
straight backed, with every rustle and sniff. One night as we
were going to bed I saw that the receiver was not on my
bedside table, where it had lived since we'd brought Culby
home.

"Babe," I called to JJ, who was brushing his teeth in the
bathroom, "where's the monitor?"

He tapped his toothbrush on the edge of the sink and
stepped into the bedroom, "Doll, we have to talk about that.
It's making you crazy, and you need to get some sleep. So I
put it away."

"What do you mean you put it away? Where is it? We
need it, it's not making me crazy," I said rapidly, my voice
rising an octave, as something just below panic filled my
chest, "It makes me more comfortable knowing that I can
hear him and —"

"Sara," he said calmly, putting one arm around me and
gesturing with the other toward the shared wall that
separated our room from the nursery, "he's literally on the
other side of that wall."

"I know, but —"

"Doll, I promise, if he wakes up we'll hear him. Trust
me." He was right, of course. And I did trust him, he had an
instinct for fatherhood that I found mysterious, and more
than a little comforting.

~

Two years later, my cell phone rang as we rolled off the ferry that had carried us across Puget Sound, on our way to spend Thanksgiving with my parents, in the small town on the tip of the Olympic Peninsula where they had retired several years earlier. JJ was driving, and Culby was sound asleep in his carseat, folded into one of those origami shapes that only small children are capable of assuming, an occasional soft snore leaking out.

"Babe!" I exclaimed, turning to him as I ended the call, and startling Culby awake, "We have another son!"

Charlie was ten days old.

The rest of of that drive was filled with happy tears, and many many calls — to my parents to ask if they could keep Culby while we went to Guatemala to meet Charlie, to the airline to book the soonest possible flights, to my partners to arrange coverage for my patients, to family and friends to share our joy. By the time we rounded the curve of my parents' driveway, everything was in place.

We called him Baby Big Eyes. Because his tiny little face really was all eyes, reminiscent of one of those Margaret Keane prints from the '70s. His irises were the color of a gourmand's darkest chocolate confection, nearly indistinguishable from the black pupils at their core, and he watched the world around him with an almost disconcerting intensity in-between feedings. I hadn't doubted JJ this time, when a woman entered the lobby of the Camino Real hotel carrying a small bundle, and he proclaimed, "There he is! There's our son!" I knew he was right, the pull of the Red Thread left no doubt. And when I held Charlie in my arms for the first time, my heart wrapping itself around him, melting into all his nooks and crannies, I felt the last piece of our family puzzle slide into place.

We spent the week on the eat-sleep-poop-repeat merry-go-round of the newborn, entirely charmed by all of it. I was much more comfortable this time around, having managed to shepherd Culby through his first two years without doing irreparable damage, but my confidence would never rival JJ's. His ease with children of all ages was enviable, but also slightly nerve-racking when it occasionally bordered on cockiness — like when I came out to the hotel pool one morning to see him standing in the hot tub with Charlie nestled into a sling across his chest.

"JJ — what are you doing?" I cried, dashing toward him, "Get out of there! What if he slipped out?"

"Don't worry Doll, he's not going to slip out," he laughed, raising both arms over his head, "look, no hands." I could've killed him then and there.

When Charlie was born, I was working a regular schedule of seven days on, followed by seven days off, so every few weeks, I was able to go down and spend an enchanted week with him, as the paperwork wended its way through the bureaucracy. Most of the time it was just the two of us, but occasionally we would have a visit from a local friend, or JJ's sister Kate, who was in the Peace Corps nearby. My mom and sister even came with me for one visit, and we took turns wearing him in his sling (which, it should be said, he never once slipped out of) during leisurely meals and afternoons by the pool.

My heart soared every time I arrived and took him into my arms, marveling at how much he'd grown since I'd held him last, at how much more alert and engaged he was, and it plummeted every time I had to hand him back to his adoring foster mother at the end of the week. JJ had other commitments, and hadn't been able to join me for the first few trips, but he and Culby would be coming next time, I explained, as she tucked him gently into his car seat. I took a deep breath as they drove away, tried to pull myself together so as not to be an unraveled mess in the taxi that would take me to Antigua, where I was to have dinner with friends before my flight home in the morning. I suspect I was not terribly successful though, because the driver was giving me sympathetic looks in the review mirror all the way there.

My friend's phone rang just after I arrived at her house about an hour later, and I heard her exclaim, "JJ! Is everything okay?" I leapt to my feet and ran across the house to her side, my heart pounding, *Something terrible must have happened, why else would he call?* She handed me the phone, and had I been paying any attention at all I would probably have noticed the sparkle in her eye and the smile on her lips, but I was blinded by red hot fear.

"JJ, what's wrong?" I didn't mean to yell, but the words shot out of their own volition.

"Don't get on the plane, Doll!" he said, the excitement in his voice causing my heart to flip over itself. "The final embassy appointment is the day after tomorrow!"

The emotional whiplash forced me to the floor, my mind struggling to reel in the terror and unspool the joy, it was taking a minute to disentangle the two.

"For real?" I asked.

"For real," he said.

"Well," I paused, to take a deep breath and clear the emotion from my throat, "I promise not to smash his head into anything."

18

SECOND FALL

That fall, all three of us went back to school.
Charlie was in fifth grade, and he had a
wonderful teacher. Mr. P was the kind of person
whose creativity and humor encourages curiosity and
instills a love of learning that continues to serve his students
long after they've left his classroom, the kind of teacher you
thank at your college graduation. Personally, he won my
heart when he used *The Princess Bride* as a lesson in irony
— it was one of JJ's favorite movies, he'd known every line.

Charlie would come bounding out of school every day,
wearing a paper crown or carrying an intricate popsicle
stick bridge, dried bits of glue on his hands and flecks of
glitter in his hair. "Mom! Mr. P said..." he would begin his
report breathlessly, handing me his backpack and lunchbox
to sherpa home. It was his last year in elementary school; his
last year in the land of crayons and safety scissors, of
playdates and stuffed animals, of sing-alongs and reading
aloud. I didn't realize how much I would miss it. I wish I
had, I would have savored it more.

Culby was in his second year at the middle school that

was conveniently located one block from our house. It had been abrupt and disorienting, the transition from fifth to sixth grade the year before: Navigating between classrooms in a much bigger building, with a different teacher for every subject, changing expectations and increasing responsibilities, real homework and actual deadlines; not to mention the raging hormones, the social obstacle courses, the fundamental shift from *little kid* to *tween* with all the attendant soul-searching and place-seeking. Anyone who has survived it knows that middle school is a quagmire. It was a lot to expect of an eleven-year-old whose world had just exploded.

He was overwhelmed, and became adept at flying under the radar, wrapped up quietly in his grief. He was at risk of slipping through the cracks, and I feared that I alone, could not provide enough of a safety net. He needed to spend his days in a place where he could heal his heart and find his legs. So, in the middle of his seventh grade year he switched to a much smaller school, with a focus on project based learning, and community engagement.

The building was open and airy, filled with light from the wall of windows that framed a perfect view of Mt Hood in the distance. Children's artwork covered the walls, and a beehive hummed on the terrace. There was a science lab where students learned the laws of physics from an actual physicist, and comfy sofas and chairs scattered around where they could relax and focus on their studies. It felt warm and comforting and safe.

Shortly after Culby started there, I received an email from one of his teachers, letting me know that the students were working on an Activism Project for which they had been asked to choose a social cause that they felt passionately about, and wanted to explore more deeply.

Culby, she said, had chosen to focus on the immigrant community.

"Culby," I said, as the boys and I waited for our milkshakes in the neighborhood ice cream shop, the only customers on a blustery winter afternoon, "Ms. D said you chose the immigrant community for your Activism Project?" His eyes lit up and he nodded as the bell over the door tinkled and a young couple with a toddler came in out of the rain. "That's great," I said, handing him his treat. "Tell me about why you picked that topic."

He thought for a moment, eyes squinting slightly, lips pursed, then he said, "Well Mom, I'm Guatemalan. And when I hear our president calling my people rapists and murderers, it really hurts."

Charlie looked up at me, with eyes too wise for his years, and added, "Yeah, it hurts a lot."

I felt a searing pain in my very core then, deep and primal. *My children carry this. They carry it alone, and I can't protect them from it.* I had hoped that I could keep them safe in our fortress, that they wouldn't pick up on it. I had wondered what I would say if they did... it's complicated, being the white mother of children of color. The instinct to protect our children is potent — that's how we humans are designed, after all. And if it were possible to keep them shielded from the brutality of racism forever, I would pour all of myself into doing just that. But our world is as it is. And a shield is not enough.

"I know, my love," I said, swallowing hard.

"So I figure," Culby said as he sat down, "if it hurts *me* that much, it must feel so much worse for *them*, and that makes me want to help them."

My heart swelled with love and pride and admiration,

for the young man my son was growing into. I cherished this glimpse of who he would be in the world.

"That's beautiful, Culby. And so very like your dad, to take something painful and make something good out of it," I said. "He'd be really proud of you."

"Excuse me," the woman who had entered earlier was approaching us with a smile. "I'm sorry, I wasn't trying to eavesdrop, but I couldn't help overhearing your conversation, and I just have to say something," her eyes were kind, and she spoke directly to Culby and Charlie. "As another American, I just have to tell you I am so sorry that you have to experience that. I am horrified by what's happening at the border, and I just want to be sure you know that the people in your community do *not* feel that way."

Tears spilled over, sliding down my cheeks as the boys smiled in response. "Thanks," they said in unison. "Thank you," I squeaked, "You're exactly why I love our Portland bubble!"

～

Meanwhile, I had started an online graduate program in Global Health with Johns Hopkins. It was rigorous, fast-paced, and challenging. And it forced me to begin slowly spinning all the fuzz that filled my mind into threads, to organize them, the makings of a tapestry.

I kept a bullet journal, which is kind of like a planner except you start with a blank notebook and then spend countless hours drawing daily, weekly, and monthly calendars and associated to-do lists yourself, preferably with color-coded fine tip pens and a corresponding legend in the front, with the index. Then, every week, you reprint each task from the monthly calendar to the weekly calendar and again to the daily calendar. And once a task is finally completed, you cross it off three times. It's a rather ridiculous system, if you think about it, the amount of time spent creating and maintaining the book could well be used to complete some of those very tasks. But I found the ritual, in itself, to be comforting. Orienting. The act of starting with a blank page and putting some structure to it, made time more real somehow. Tasks more concrete. Slowed my mind down, allowed it to focus.

I felt inspired and invigorated, and I dove into learning about global epidemiology, statistical analysis, community health programs, supply chain management, SMART analysis. It was like brain candy. It was a relief to focus on something other than our grief, and it was utterly delicious. But, as with all things delicious, there is the risk of over indulgence. I struggled with balance — always vaguely surprised, when I looked up at the end of a day spent studying, that dinner wasn't ready and waiting for us in the kitchen.

That was the fall we coined the term *Free Range Dinner*, and Charlie learned how to scramble an egg.

It was also the fall that the Democrats won back the House of Representatives, and Brett Kavanaugh was confirmed to the Supreme Court. That the UN panel on Climate Change warned we had 12 years to the point-of-no-return, and a 7.5 magnitude earthquake and subsequent tsunami killed over 1600 people in Indonesia. That fires raged, from Paradise to Queensland, and Ebola threatened Congo. All of which passed through me, some bits lingering for a moment, even if at a distance. I couldn't hold it yet, but I was beginning to see it.

19

KRYPTONITE

(2007-2013)

A t first I didn't understand why he wasn't starting the car. I was bouncing up and down in the passenger seat myself, unable to contain my ebullience after leaving the oncologist's office; but he just sat there, gripping the steering wheel and staring straight ahead.

"Babe," I stopped bouncing and turned to him, "why aren't you starting the car?" I was stunned to see that he was weeping as he sat there, still as stone, the rivulets tracing a path down his cheeks and dripping from his chin to form twin pools on the collar of his black leather jacket. In all our years together, it was only the second time I had seen him cry. I was confused.

The oncologist had just told us that JJ'd had the best possible outcome. It had been five years, and with no evidence of persistent or recurrent tumor, he was considered cancer-free. His odds of a recurrence were now thought to be the same as his odds of a second primary tumor. No more MRIs, no more chemotherapy, no more oncology appointments. He would have to continue his anti-seizure medication of course, but he'd not had a seizure in over a year, and he even had his drivers license back. It was over!

He turned to face me, his expression tortured.

"The easy part was figuring out how to die, Doll. The hard part is figuring out how to live. Now. With this different brain."

Ultimately, JJ had completed his Masters degree, but not his PhD; it turns out science requires very specific language, and that was his kryptonite. He had found his words again, but only to a point — although this was really only apparent when he was trying to describe things such as the the the complex genome of the soil bacterium *Sinorhizobium meliloti,* and its symbiotic relationship with alfalfa and other legumes. But when you're a scientist, it's not enough for *you* to know what you're trying to say, the ability to communicate your findings within the strict parameters of accepted scientific norms is required. And he agonized over the struggle to translate his knowledge and ideas into that shared language, forced to accept that intellectual capacity alone was not sufficient. Forced to set aside his passion, to seek a new purpose. To gather the shards of his dreams, and piece them back together into unexpected silhouettes.

And as he did, he made a conscious choice every single day, to strive to be a better man than he had been the day before. He didn't always succeed of course, but until his dying day, he never stopped trying. Which is more than most of us can say. And one of the things I loved most about him.

I had finished residency and was working as a hospitalist, so I could support us financially. And JJ was a natural with kids — not just our own either, as evidenced by the gang of neighborhood boys that regularly appeared at our front door.

"Is JJ here?" they would ask, waiting patiently while I called him.

"Honey, your friends are here!"

JJ ultimately chose to be our full-time parent, and in that, he found his purpose. And frankly, he did a much better job than I could have, and whined much less than I fear I would have been inclined to do. It was not an easy transition for him, though — at that time, and especially in Spokane, there were no other Full Time Dads. He was an oddity. But he embraced it, and at the playgroups and music circles, when someone would call out "Moms, over here!" he would clear his throat, and remind them with a smile, that there was a dad there, too.

~

"Doll, I think it's time to move back to Portland," JJ said one night, as we sat down to dinner. To our surprise, it had been ten years since we'd made the temporary move to Spokane.

"For real?" I asked. We'd had a false start a few years earlier but had ultimately decided to wait, mostly out of laziness. We had a nice life in Spokane — close friends, convenient travel, mountains and rivers nearby. Our house was comfortable, there were no traffic jams, the schools were good. It was easy.

But it was never Home.

Charlie would be starting kindergarten, and Culby

would be in second grade. They had spent their whole lives in Spokane, and if we were going to uproot them, now was the time. So in June of 2013, we packed up the beige house with the white trim, on the corner lot with the big maple tree in front, and moved back home, to Portland.

20

SECOND CHRISTMAS

I put up the Christmas tree the day after Thanksgiving that year. It would be our first Christmas at home without JJ, and I was determined to embrace the Holiday Spirit. We would be jolly, dammit.

"Daddy has to be with us, by the fireplace!" Culby and Charlie declared, handing me JJ's box, "And he needs his hat!" His hat. It was a three foot long stocking cap, with red and white stripes and a fluffy pom pom on the end. I had knitted it for him, at his request, and he had worn it with glee every time he went out between Thanksgiving and Christmas. So he watched over us from the mantle in his beautiful box, a swirl of grain curled up in a grin below his holiday hat, stretched neatly over the top, pom pom dangling cheerfully on the end.

We listened to Christmas music while we decorated the tree and put up fairy lights, replaced paintings with wreaths and hung our stockings by the fire. I hesitated, unsure if I should hang JJ's stocking — would it be too stark a reminder? But wouldn't its absence be even worse? Would it splinter the delicate ice beneath our feet and send us plunging back into the depths? It was exceedingly brittle that layer, prone to sudden shattering, almost always without warning, and shocking in its violence. I lived in fear of the cracks.

But the boys looked at me like I had three heads when I asked what they preferred, "Of course you have to hang it up, Mom," they said with a roll of their eyes. "Obviously."

And it struck me then, stopped me dead in my tracks — I was afraid of the *next trip* to the bottom. By definition, that must mean I was not always *there*.

Huh.

I made cioppino for Christmas Eve dinner, and as I was laying out the crackers for the crab claws and the tiny silver seafood forks, I paused at the end of the table where I usually sat: *This is exactly where JJ was, on our last Christmas Eve.* He washed over me, at once filling me up and hollowing me out, and I stood there with my eyes closed, remembering how we had pulled the hospital bed up to the end of the table that night, raising the back so he was sitting upright. How he had joined us in a toast, and even nibbled on some food, before dozing off, surrounded by the score of his life. Remembering how he had smiled the whole time.

Late that night, after the stockings had been stuffed, and a bite taken from each of Santa's cookies, I sat alone with him by the fire. Me in my Christmas PJs, he in his holiday hat. We talked for hours.

Christmas Day was surreal, I moved through it gingerly. Everything was just slightly off-center, familiar and alien. Comforting and precarious. Filled with sudden laughter and hidden landmines. Like when I was gathering spices for the roast and came across an old pickle jar with an index card taped to it that read: *THE* (underlined three times)

Prime Rib Rub, in his distinct hand. I saw him clearly, standing there surrounded by a dozen spice jars, lids in a pile to the side. Face focused, measuring precisely, referring intently to the recipe between perfectly leveled scoops. I saw him go to the desk in the mud room and pull out the center drawer, the one that sticks, and extract an index card. Grab a black sharpie from the mug with DAD painted on it that Culby made for him one Father's Day. I saw him bending over the island in the kitchen, underlining the *THE* three times, with a grin, and taping the card carefully to the jar.

This jar.

I tucked it back in the cupboard, a talisman.

We cleared away the mountains of crumpled wrapping paper left over from the morning frenzy and put both leaves in the dining room table, with two card tables extending it into the living room in order to fit the whole family. David tried to teach me how to use the smoker, but really just ended up cooking the perfect prime rib himself, and Kelly brought her magical celery root mash. The house was full, busy and loud, like it always had been when JJ was alive — when at least once a week he'd say, "I'm throwing something on the smoker, Doll, see if anyone wants to join us," and we'd have a Family Dinner with whoever was around.

It felt good, cheerful even — the kiddos enthralled with their new toys, a football game on in the living room, the hum of a holiday feast being prepared. But intermittently, and unpredictably, my very center would begin to dilate, and a vacuous hole would start to grow. The lip of it would creep outward, luring me with its promise of quiet numbness, of the comfort to be found in the familiar weight of my grief. Tempting me to jump in, to sink down to the very bottom and curl up into a ball, hold my breath. But it was different now, because even when I succumbed, even when I felt it in every single cell, when the weight of it left me gasping, I could somehow manage to pull myself up enough to get my mouth above the water for a minute, and suck in a breath. That was progress.

~

I was dreading January 11. The Second Anniversary. I was afraid I might have used up all my reserves over the holidays, that I might not have it in me to pull us out of the hole this time. I felt frayed and fragile, unprepared. But Time doesn't care, it won't wait for you to be ready. And so I woke up at exactly 3:00 again. Rolled over and stared at the clock. Probed the memories, each stab of pain proof that he was real.

We survived that day, snuggled up on the sofa in our PJs, eating junk and watching movies. And as I lay curled up on his side of the bed late that night, weeping into the pillow made from his favorite jeans and laughing at how much he would love that I was crying on his butt, I thought, *Well, that's two down. One more to go, I suppose.*

~

"I am not a *single* parent, I am an *only* parent," the woman sitting across from me said emphatically. "I don't have someone else to take my kids every other weekend, or pick them up from soccer practice if I have to work late. I'm on deck 24/7, 365 days a year. And it pisses me off when people say things like *Oh I know just how you feel, it's so hard being a single mom.* Like it's even remotely the same thing." *She has a point,* I thought, as I sipped my martini.

It was my first meeting of the "Widows Club", and there were ten or so of us, seated around an enormous table that filled the back room of a popular restaurant. A friend of mine whose husband had died just as we moved back to Portland, leaving her with a broken heart and two young children, had invited me along. She introduced me to the other mourning members when we arrived.

"It's nice to meet you," I said to the man holding out his hand in greeting. I glanced up at him as we shook hands, and for an instant he came into sharp focus for me. Which threw me for a loop, because I still didn't have the bandwidth for strangers. They typically moved around my orbit as amorphous blurs, interactions brief and transactional. It passed in a flash, but left me vaguely confused and slightly nauseous. *Did I just notice that he has blue eyes?*

As we went around the table, introducing ourselves and sharing a bit of our stories, it struck me how young we all were, to be widowed. How most of us still had children to raise, how we all faced a future that looked nothing like the one we had envisioned, how the prospect of growing old alone had suddenly become our collective reality. It was at once comforting, and devastating. Tom had lost his wife to breast cancer, and his 12-year-old daughter was struggling. Marie's husband had died of esophageal cancer, Amy's of colon cancer, Lily's of multiple myeloma. They all had children in elementary school. Some of us had nursed our partner through a long illness, others had been blindsided by a sudden diagnosis and a quick passing. All of us bore the scars.

Will, of the blue eyes, sat across from me. "My wife

died of a brain tumor almost exactly one year ago," he said softly, snapping me out of myself. "I thought I'd feel better after I got past the first anniversary, but I actually feel worse, and I don't understand..." In a flash, I was right back there, in the darkness. The pit in my stomach left no room for the sushi I'd just ordered.

"I'm a year ahead of you Will," I said, wanting to reach out and take his hand, but the table was wider than my arms were long. "My husband died of a brain tumor too, almost exactly two years ago." He looked up, and the suffering in his eyes made my soul ache. "And after the first anniversary was actually my darkest time, I felt the same way. I couldn't figure out why I wasn't *better*. I thought it must be me, that there was something magical about surviving the Year of Firsts, and that I should just be able to snap out of it."

"And how about now?" he asked, leaning forward and looking at me intently, just as I had looked at Carrie that day at The Center. Searching.

"Well," I spoke slowly, "I've learned there's nothing magical about the second anniversary either, but also that the lows aren't as incapacitating, and don't last as long. And there are more good days in-between now. I don't think any of us will ever *get over it*, but I think that eventually we can learn how to carry it without being crushed. That's my hope, anyway."

"Cheers to that," someone said, and we raised our glasses in a toast, to hope.

~

When my phone rang I jumped to grab it. Normally I wouldn't have it on when out to dinner, but it was the first time I'd left the boys alone, and even though I was only five minutes away, I was nervous.

"Mom! Charlie cut his finger on the cheese grater and it won't stop bleeding!" It was Culby, and he sounded scared. I leapt up from my seat at the end of the table, my new position as the third or fifth or seventh wheel now, and rushed outside so as not to be that person yapping on their phone in the middle of a quiet restaurant.

"I'll come home right now," I said, trying to keep my voice calm. JJ and I had often spoken with them about how unpredictable life can be, explained that unexpected and sometimes scary things will happen, and that in those moments the most important thing is to stay calm so that you can focus on solving the problem. "Take a deep breath," we inhaled and exhaled together. "Now, go grab a paper towel and hold it on the cut, push down hard cause that'll stop the bleeding."

"Okay," I heard them tear off the towel, and Culby say to his little brother, "It's okay Charlie," as he wrapped it around the wound.

"I'm going to grab my coat and I'll be right there," I said, reaching for the restaurant door.

"That's okay Mom," Culby sounded more confident now, "we can handle it."

They took a picture and sent it to me, and I was relieved that despite what seemed like an unreasonable amount of blood, it would not require stitches. The bleeding eventually stopped, and as I was talking them through cleaning it up, selecting the appropriate sized bandage and applying it without getting the sticky part on the cut, our charming waiter appeared in the doorway, and handed me my cocktail with a sympathetic look.

"Are you sure you don't want me to come home, guys?"

I was conflicted — did they need me to be there to kiss their owies and make them better? Or, at eleven and thirteen now, did they need the room to navigate some challenges on their own? Would they feel abandoned, or empowered? What would JJ do?

"I'm okay Mom, you don't need to come home," Charlie sounded calm, "I kept a grip. And Culby's taking care of me."

Does every parent remember that moment? When their babies suddenly morph into independent entities? When out of necessity or circumstance they demonstrate for the first time their ability to navigate the unexpected? It's very disconcerting, that shift from utter dependence to semi-autonomy. I wasn't sure I was ready for it.

21

TIMOTHY LAKE

(2013)

As soon as the lake came into view, Culby and Charlie started bouncing, "When can we go on the boat, Dad? When can we go on the boat, Dad? When can we go on the boat, Dad?" Their smiles popped in and out of sight in the rearview mirror as they giggled between refrains. The boat they referred to was a sit-on-top kayak which was strapped to the roof, and JJ had promised to take them out on it first thing. At seven and five, they felt it was time to learn how to paddle it themselves, and Timothy Lake was the perfect place to learn. It sits tucked into the green folds of Mount Hood National Forest, and the campground has several sites along the shore, with others ringing two large loops that snake through the forest. The lake is smooth and sparkling, and the snowy summit of Mt Hood towers in the distance, its sharp peak occasionally softened by a few wispy cirrus clouds or a saucer shaped lenticular formation hovering motionless, snagged on the jagged sheets of rock. There is a small beach, perfect for lounging, and the water is cold but not prohibitive. It's a hidden treasure, and one of the many reasons we were happy to be back in Portland — it had only been a month, but it felt like we'd never left.

Culby and Charlie leapt from the car as soon as we came to a stop, clamoring for their bikes to be released from the rack so they could have a race, but they kept one eye on their dad at all times, and the instant JJ lifted the kayak off of the roof, they appeared at his side, "Is it time now, Dad?"

The three of them piled on, the boys faces rapt as JJ showed them how to hold the paddle, how to stroke evenly, and what happened if you only paddled on one side. Culby went first on his own, and he was a natural, his strokes were smooth, his turns well maneuvered. Charlie, for his part, had been absorbed in a frenzied swarm of crawdads devouring a very dead fish near the shore, but he eventually grew bored with the spectacle, and struck out to join his brother. Of course when he tried to scramble onto the kayak, Culby was thrown off balance, the paddle was lost, and suffice to say, chaos ensued.

That was when we explained to them that every boat has a captain, and the captain is in charge. So when you want to board a vessel, you need to inform the captain and get permission first, in order to do it safely. And when the captain tells you to do something, you do it, for the same reason. They nodded solemnly, wise now to the dangers, having survived their first shipwreck.

Kids are very literal at that age.

A short while later, Culby and Charlie were out paddling around while we watched from the shore, when we heard Culby shout imperiously, "Take me to the land!" Charlie immediately began paddling like mad, while Culby lay back, legs stretched out in front of him and crossed at the ankle, with one arm folded underneath his head and the other pointing toward the shore, like a Pharaoh being spirited across the Nile.

"So..." JJ said slowly, once Charlie had fulfilled his edict and they were both back on dry land, "let's talk for a minute, about the difference between a captain and a king..."

The next morning brought a bright blue sky, and we soaked up every glorious minute of a perfect lake day. We paddled and explored and skipped stones. The boys built forts and quickly weaponized nature — sticks became swords and rocks became bombs, which required quite a bit of active parenting. We hunted tadpoles and blew Charlie's mind when we explained how they would eventually grow legs and morph into frogs. He was skeptical to say the least. It was the kind of fun you have when your kids are small, and everything is new and exciting.

Late that afternoon when JJ and the boys came in from a paddle, sun-kissed and windblown, JJ had a disconcerted look on his face. "Are you okay, Babe?" I asked. He looked at me, as if to consider his response, but then just nodded and ducked into the tent. I waited for a while but when he didn't emerge, I followed him in and found him sitting on his sleeping bag, focused intently on his hands which rested on his legs before him.

"J, are you okay? What's happening?" I asked.

"I smelled a horrible smell when we were out on the boat Doll, but the boys didn't smell it." He was speaking slowly, deliberately, "My mouth tastes like metal. And before, I couldn't find the words..." It was his first seizure in years. He looked up at me sheepishly, and I realized he was holding his medication box.

"Babe, have you been taking your meds?" I tried not to sound accusatory, but I probably failed.

"Mostly," he said, holding up the med box with the day's pills still rattling around inside.

"Well, I'm sure that's all it is," I said, resisting the urge to scold him.

22

THIRD SPRING

Charlie has always bounced. As a toddler, he was that kid who knew no fear — he would leap onto impossibly complicated climbing structures at the park for example, navigating his way to the top like a mountain goat before we had a chance to grab him, and then laughing as he nimbly worked his way back down, utterly delighted with himself. When he did fall, on occasion, he would spring right back up and be fully engrossed in something else by the time we had sprinted to his side, always slightly confused by the panicked look on our faces. He never understood what the big deal was — if you fell down, you just got back up and kept going, right?

When he was four, he fell out of his second-story bedroom window, landing with a thud at the feet of a young landscaper who was busy hacking through the frozen earth of early spring, attempting to plant a rhododendron. The young landscaper reacted like any human being would when a child falls from the sky: he scooped him up and rushed around to the front door in search of a parent, frantically ringing the bell and calling for JJ, oblivious to the risk of spinal cord injury. That poor guy, I suspect he may have been the most traumatized of us all.

I was in the middle of rounds, on the third floor medical unit, when JJ called, "Doll, Charlie fell out of his bedroom window."

I froze mid-stride, blocking the entrance to the nurses station, "To the ground?!" I replied, probably quite loudly, which I think is how the rumor that my house burned down got started. "I'll meet you in the ER."

I flew down the stairs, gripping my heart in my hands, terrified that I would trip and drop it, shatter it. The doctor part of me remained detached, calmly running down the list of potential injuries and what workup would be required. The mother part of me could not stop shaking. Then they arrived in a flurry, and all of the things that you do when someone comes to the ER having fallen from a second story window were done — x-rays, ultrasounds, neurologic exams, bloodwork — but there were no broken bones, no wounds needing sutures, no internal damage, no evidence of a head injury. The child literally did not have a scratch on him. JJ and I, however, were permanently scarred.

It was only after Charlie's tears had dried, and our blood pressure had normalized that it occurred to me to ask the Doc taking care of him if she'd mind removing those stitches in his head from ten days ago...

～

"Mom!" Culby shouted as he ran into the kitchen where the grownups were clearing the lunch dishes while the kiddos played outside, "Charlie fell off the zip-line, and he hurt his arm really bad!"

It was our third Spring Break as a tricycle, and we were

in the English countryside with my cousin and her two sons. We'd taken the train from London together to visit our other cousin and spend the day with her family at their farm, part of what my boys dubbed "Cousinpalooza". The next leg would involve a train to Paris where we would meet JJ's brother and his family, including three more cousins, and then travel with them back to their home in Germany, where we would spend a week exploring ancient ruins and eating schnitzel.

Charlie was bustled into the house surrounded by the cousin guard, all wearing doleful expressions as the wounded soldier tried to hold back his tears and explain what had happened, "I was going so fast," he hiccuped, "I got scared and let go." He was supporting his left arm gingerly with his right, and trying his hardest to remain stoic as I examined it.

"Can you move your hand like this?"

"Yes."

"Can you feel me touching your fingers?"

"Yes."

"Can you make a fist?"

"Yes."

Here, I feel the need for a disclaimer — I am not an orthopedist, nor am I a pediatrician. I am an internist, which means my expertise is in taking care of *adults*. When they're *sick*. On the *inside*. Just to be clear.

I wasn't sure what to do: did we need to take the train back to London and find an ER for an x-ray, or not? I took photos, and texted them to a trusted colleague back in the States, "...it's swollen and tender over the ulnar styloid, but he has full range of motion, neurovascularly intact, no gross deformity, what do you think?"

By the time she replied, "I'd just wrap it up and give

him some ibuprofen," Charlie was already back outside playing soccer with his cousins.

When we arrived in Paris, we had already acquired an elastic bandage and matching sling, and Charlie's standard response whenever I asked how his arm felt was, "Awesome!" He did not complain once as we explored the Louvre and the Eiffel Tower. Did not emit a moan or a whine or a grumble as he joined Culby and their cousins, running and laughing and sword-fighting their way through Germany, although I did have to cut his schnitzel for him.

It wasn't until we got back home that he turned to me and said, "Mom, my wrist still hurts."

I looked at him in disbelief, "But, I've been asking you constantly how it feels, and you keep saying *Awesome!*"

"I know," he said, looking down at his feet, "but it didn't hurt when I was having fun..."

When the pediatric orthopedist showed us the x-ray, the break was obvious, even to my internist's eye. It was what we call a green-stick fracture, because the bone bends and splinters on one side like a small tree branch would, without breaking completely. They usually happen in young children, whose bones are softer and more flexible than they will eventually become. Whose everything is, I suppose.

"Mom," Charlie said with a sly grin, his arm now safely secured in a red and green striped cast, "can we stop for some guilt-McDonald's on the way home?" I looked at him in the review mirror, eyebrows raised. "I mean, you did let me run around Europe for a week with a broken arm," he continued with a giggle. McDonald's had been their little secret with their dad, they would stop there occasionally on the way to go fishing or skiing or kayaking, and they knew that I would have been appalled, so they just never mentioned it. It only came out after JJ died, and I confess, my stance softened a bit once I found myself responsible for 21 meals a week. Also, the guilt was real.

It's one of the hardest things about being an only parent, the isolation in times of crisis. No matter whose council you seek, you carry your children alone.

∾

That was the spring of the College Admissions Scandal, when wealthy and sometimes famous parents were accused of paying vast sums of money as well as outright lying and cheating to secure competitive university spots for their children, often without their knowledge. Culby was deeply offended by this, particularly on behalf of those kids who were unaware that they had been accepted under false pretenses, "I mean, that's just saying to your kid that you don't think they can succeed on their own. That's not good parenting," he said.

He was beginning to discover himself at his new school, where they encouraged social awareness and open debate on topical issues. It surprised me, for example, when he came home one day, full of admiration for the New Zealand government. They had passed a ban on automatic and assault rifles just six days after the Christchurch mass-shooting, when the murder of 51 people and the wounding of 49 others had been live-streamed on social media. "Why haven't we passed a law like that?" he wondered.

One day towards the end of the year, Culby and I pulled into the driveway after school, but instead of leaping out of the car and rushing to jump on his bike / grab his soccer ball / turn on his PS4, he sat in the passenger seat looking down at his hands.

"What's up, Culbs?" I asked. "Is everything okay?"

He reached into his bag and extracted a small jar filled with a mixture of spices, and an intricately folded card, "This is for you, Mom, for your birthday," he said softly.

"Oh Sweetheart, that's lovely, thank you so much," I said with a smile. But as he turned to hand them to me, a big fat tear escaped and slid down his cheek.

"Everyone was making Father's Day gifts," he said, a quiver in his voice. "I guess I'm glad it's your birthday too, so I could make it for you instead." My smile wilted, my heart did too. This was a first, the public schools were dismissed for the summer well before Father's Day, but his new school had an extended year.

"That must have been really hard," I said, reaching over and taking him in my arms. "Did you feel supported at least? Did your teachers talk to you about it?"

He shook his head silently, wiping away another tear. No. Not one single adult had taken a moment to check-in. To ask this heartsick child if it might be painful to be tasked with creating a gift for his dead father. A gift that could never be given. To consider that it might just rip the scabs from his wounded heart, and leave him bleeding and bereft. Not one single adult had demonstrated even a modicum of compassion or empathy as he suffered through that day.

Rage set my insides on fire. I felt my face flush, my heart rate jump, my stomach churn. *That's the whole reason he's at that Tiny School! I've talked to his teachers so many times, they know his story, they know he's grieving and fragile. And they* don't *know that my birthday happens to be coming up also — I mean, what did they think he was going to do with this gift?!*

"But Grace made me feel better," Culby said, with a hint of a smile through his tears. "She said she thought it must be hard making a present for my dad when he's not here and I can't give it to him." Grace was one of his classmates, a remarkably self-possessed seventh-grade girl, with a degree of insight and compassion well beyond her years. "She asked if I was okay, and she sat with me while we were working on it. That helped."

I don't think I have ever felt so grateful. To anyone. For anything.

That night I sat down and wrote two letters. The first, to Culby's teachers, asking what they had been thinking and how they could have been so callous (and to be honest, I had to write several drafts before I could send it without risk of being expelled from the school for profanity). Their response gave me pause: "We didn't want to bring it up, because we didn't know how he was feeling, and we didn't want to upset him."

I was gobsmacked. Rather than asking him how he was feeling, recognizing an opportunity for growth and healing, creating a teaching moment by modeling compassion and empathy, they chose silence. Weren't these professional educators? Experts on child development? Didn't they understand that ignoring Culby's pain only served to increase it?

But then I realized, it spoke to something bigger than the Tiny School, shined a light on our society's collective dysfunction around grief. We are so often paralyzed when confronted with loss, fearful that we will say the wrong thing, that despite the best of intentions we will inflict more pain than we relieve. So we say nothing, rather than risk making it worse. But in the end, that silence only serves to further isolate the one who suffers, to leave them alone with their grief. It tells them that their pain is taboo, not to be discussed — because it makes people uncomfortable, and that's just not polite.

What I have learned is this: It's always better to say "I don't know what to say," than to say nothing at all.

The second letter was to Grace's parents. I wanted to give them a glimpse of who their daughter was as she moved through the world beyond their sight, of the impact she had on those in her orbit, because don't all parents wonder about that? I wanted them to know that they were raising a young woman who's reaction to another's pain was not to shy away from it, but to move toward it, offering comfort and kindness. I wanted Grace to know too, that her small gesture would have a profound and lasting impact. That just bearing witness to another's suffering, acknowledging it, being brave enough to sit with it, is an act of courage and compassion. Of humanity. Of love.

23

HUBRIS

(2013)

D r. V wanted to get an MRI. I rolled my mind's eye, *Okay, New Neurologist,* I thought, *I understand he's a new patient for you, and yes, he does have a history of brain cancer, and yes, he did just have a little breakthrough seizure, but really — it was just because he wasn't taking his meds consistently.* I sighed on the inside. *But I get it,* I thought, in my most patronizing tone, *You just need to reassure yourself, so okay...*

We weren't worried. We were protected by hubris. We knew that we were safely on the other side, that we had survived. Dr. V had only just met JJ, but we knew the secret — that JJ was magic, the exception, he had proven it over and over again throughout the nine and a half years since that first seizure. And we had done the work after all, fulfilled our part of the unwritten contract with the Universe. We had dug deep and found our grit, we had unearthed the lessons buried there and incorporated them into our fiber, we had grown stronger and more gentle, our compassion expanded, our world view broadened, our priorities clarified. We had come out on the other side wiser, closer, better. The war was over, and we had won.

But then we heard the Universe whisper, "Oh yeah, you think you learned so much? Grew so much? Evolved so much? Well, now it's time to walk the walk." And it was all I could do to send a stunned text to our loved ones,

"The Bitch is back."

The boys named it Yucky. The tumor. Because we wanted them to have a way to think about it and talk about it that separated it from their dad himself, even though it was part of him. They were five and seven years old the day we sat with them in the freshly painted living room of our new home in Portland, explaining that Daddy had some cells in his brain that had lost their "off" switch. They sat silent and wide eyed while we talked about the medicine that Daddy would take, how it might make him feel tired sometimes, how it was really strong and its job was to banish Yucky.

"Is Daddy going to die?" Charlie asked, with the frank innocence of the five-year-old.

JJ and I looked at each other blankly, incapable of summoning any words at all, let alone the right ones, I mean what do you say to that? And then Culby said matter-of-factly,

"Everything dies, Charlie."

24

THIRD SUMMER

I looked up from my biostatistics homework when I heard Culby admonish his little brother from the other side of my bedroom door, "Quiet, Charlie! Mom's studying. Don't bother her!"

"But I'm hungry! When's it gonna be dinner?" Charlie whined.

"I dunno, have some cereal or something," Culby advised, with the authority of the newly minted teenager. Charlie sighed dramatically and stomped away, the pictures on the wall rattling.

Oh my God, it's almost 8:00! Their bedtime was 8:30, no wonder they were hangry. I had been so engrossed in the use of probability distributions that I had completely lost track of time. Again. *Parent of the Year here,* I thought as I leapt from my bed and threw the door open, "I'm so sorry guys! I didn't realize it was so late!"

"Mom!" They lit up instantly, "We're STARVING!"

I felt a sharp stabbing pain in the center of my chest then. The irony of my own children, hungry and waiting to be fed, while I focused on learning what I needed to know in order to help *other* people, slapped me across the face. Hard.

~

Charlie would be starting sixth grade the following year, and wanted to attend the Arts Middle School in our district, where enrollment was by lottery. For the required Open House, he wore a special outfit: a red tee shirt and a pair of his dad's athletic shorts which were really culottes on him, chartreuse sloth-printed knee socks, orange and turquoise soccer slides, and to pull it all together — a black Harry Potter wizard's robe. As we entered the old brick building there were student-greeters welcoming the potential families, and one of them immediately turned to Charlie and exclaimed, "Hi! I love your robe! Is that Ravenclaw House?" Charlie broke into a grin that did not leave his face for days. And as we walked back to the car later that evening, he turned to me and said excitedly, "Mom — I think I've found my people!"

I couldn't have agreed more.

~

She was sitting in the row right behind me at Charlie's fifth grade graduation, brunette curls bouncing. It still made me giggle when I remembered our one and only exchange, at the Open House two years earlier:

"And your husband is..."

"Dead."

She had made it through two whole school years without ever looking at me again — I felt badly for her that she'd happened to end up right behind me now, wondered if it made her uncomfortable. I hadn't noticed her during the Clap Out or when the adults formed the tunnel for Charlie and his classmates to run through as we cheered. But there she was, porcelain blue doll eyes blinking and, it seemed, making a concerted effort not to land on me. I turned around, hoping to catch her eye so that I could give her a smile, let her know it was all okay, but whatever it is that lives just beyond my left ear still held her attention, and she never did meet my gaze.

That now-familiar piece of me was there too, floating off in the distance. The one taking note of all the missing moments. Tucking them away for later, when I could curl up alone with the void of it all.

This is it, Babe, no more littles — they're both in middle school now...

"They're still little, Doll," he whispered.

To celebrate, Charlie wanted to go to Salty's on the river for crab, and I was happy to oblige — frankly I was relieved, I'd been bracing myself for another trip to Oaks Amusement Park. Brian and Meg joined us along with their three kids, and we sat at a long table with a banquette on one side, light streaming in through a wall of windows that opened onto the river. Charlie wore a plastic lobster bib that covered his torso completely, and his face lit up in delight when his plate arrived, bearing the biggest crab claw any of us had ever seen, "It's as big as half of my arm!" he said in awe, holding it up for comparison — indeed, it reached from his shoulder to his elbow, and he devoured it joyfully.

We laughed and chatted and reminisced, tears glazing my eyes the whole time. They weren't the grab-you-by-the-throat-and-split-you-in-half kind of tears, though, like at Culby's graduation two years earlier. No, these were more gentle. Nostalgic even. The warmth of happy memories was nestling in among the pain, loosening it up, making room for new ones.

~

I remember that summer as a healing time. Soothing. A salve on scorched skin.

Culby and Charlie spent a week camping in the Rocky Mountains with JJ's dad, their Uncle Vijay, and two of their cousins. It was a chance for them to share their thoughts and memories, for the boys to hear stories about their dad's antics as a boy, for them all to find comfort in the warmth of shared grief and the majesty of Nature. It was an adventure that JJ would have relished, a trip he had done many times himself. Their dad had loved those mountains, they felt closer to him there.

While they were gone, I spent a weekend in Colorado with two of my oldest and dearest friends. We grew up together, and have carried each other's secrets for over 40 years. It's the kind of friendship that is impervious to time or distance, that shows up when needed regardless of convenience; the kind of friendship that fills you up, that sustains you. I came away feeling buttressed and rejuvenated, reinforced. Grateful.

That summer we celebrated the 50th wedding anniversary of JJ's parents, too. It was a joyous occasion. And momentous. I reflexively braced myself for the gut-punch that day. I was prepared, ready for the vice to tighten around my heart, for my stomach to churn and my eyes to leak, as we sat at the long table breaking bread and sharing stories. When the toasts began, I clutched my napkin and took a deep breath, determined not to weep at the table.

But, it was kinder than I expected. Softer than I'd imagined. Less raw.

It was becoming easier to lean in to the happy moments. To taste joy again, if only in wisps. I was relieved to know it was possible, I'd been worried that I might've lost the knack completely.

~

We were all deeply relieved that this Labor Day weekend would not be spent dodging bald-faced hornets, as it had been the year before. Bald-faced hornets are enormous, and carnivorous, and they defend their nests with vigor. Their bodies are long and black, their faces covered with white markings, like war paint. They hunt honeybees, ripping off their heads and flying in formation back to the nest, decapitated bodies dangling from their six-jointed legs. It's gruesome, and also a bit frightening, because they can sting multiple times, and even once is outrageously painful. I learned that truth when I was stung on my thigh, which promptly grew to twice the size of its counterpart, making me look like I'd been doing isolated right-legged squats for all of my adult life.

We had not yet found a replacement for Cape Lookout, but that didn't inhibit our End of Summer Celebration. Bear Springs was just fine, as long as there were no more bald-faced hornets' nests, and no other people in the vicinity to be disturbed by our shenanigans. We were in the forest now rather than on the coast, but there was a small lake nearby, and trails to explore, and we spent a glorious day rafting on the Deschutes river. We played bocce and corn-hole and euchre. Brian set up a zipline, which provided hours of squealing laughter and, surprisingly, not a single disaster — despite the jagged shards of wood left protruding from a stump when its tree toppled over, which lay directly below the zipline, ready to impale any rider who fell at just the wrong time. Needless to say, Charlie avoided it.

I woke up at dawn on Labor Day, the rest of the camp still sound asleep, dew sparkling in the early morning sun. I was feeling reflective, seeking a minute of solitude, so I thought I'd make a cup of coffee and walk over to the big open field just across the access road, to watch the morning unfold. I opened my car door and grabbed the coffee, hit the unlock button and dropped my keys onto the driver's seat, then walked around to get the French press out of the back. The tailgate didn't open. I tried again. Nope. I rolled my eyes at myself, and went back to the driver's side door to hit unlock again. But it didn't open either. *What?* I tried the back door. No. The passenger side doors. No, and no. *Did I seriously just lock my keys in the car?* My eyes landed on the driver's seat, and there they lay, taunting me.

I'm not sure why that precise moment blindsided me so absolutely, but I instantly and thoroughly decompensated. It was as if a thousand sand bags had been released from the trees above, each one a direct hit, landing with a force that drove me right to my knees. Crushing me, squeezing all of my body's fluids out through my eyes. Unfortunately for my friend Drew, he was the only creature stirring, already up and packing his motorcycle, because he needed to get home.

"Drew," I wailed through my tears, "I locked my keys in my car and I don't know how to get them out and my phone's in there and so's my purse and there's no cell coverage to even call AAA anyway and all I want is a cup of coffee and the French press is in the car and so is the propane and so is all of our food and everyone's still asleep and JJ can't help me because he's *dead*." I sank down onto a fallen log with my face in my hands, sobbing with my whole body.

"Ummm..." Drew was at a loss. He stood beside his motorcycle, frozen in mid-packing position, hands full of gear and straps, his friend dissolving before his eyes.

JJ whispered in my ear then, "Just ride the wave, Doll."

But you're gone and I'm still here and I don't know how to do this and every time I think I'm starting to figure it out I get tripped up by something and fall right back into the hole and I'm just so tired, J...

"I know, Doll, just breathe."

Drew sat down quietly beside me, put his arm around my shoulders. Kept me tethered until I could sit upright again. I was beginning to understand, that grief is a fickle companion. Sneaky and unpredictable. Ferocious and feral. She will trick you into believing that you're almost okay, allow you some peace on a holiday or a birthday or an anniversary, for example; con you into letting your guard down by receding just enough to allow for a taste of the sweet in the bittersweet. Then, in the most casual of moments, just when you think you're safe, when you're at your most vulnerable, she will ambush you. And she will show no mercy. She will try to take you down.

Sometimes, she will succeed.

But sometimes, you will prevail. Sometimes, you will find yourself riding through the tsunami. Letting it wash over you and through you and beyond you, leaving behind a delicate residue that will slowly grow to become a trove, filled with all the beautiful bits.

25

WORD SALAD
(2013-2016)

I was standing in the kitchen trying to remember if JJ used level or heaping scoops when he measured out the coffee, when I heard him call from the bedroom where I'd left him sleeping. He was tolerating the chemo well, but it tired him out, and I had assumed the morning ritual — although I never could get the coffee to water ratio quite right.

"Shoe steak flat thing forward." *I must have misheard him.*

"What?" I called from the kitchen.

"Floor and thing in the thing." *He must still be half asleep.*

"Babe, I can't understand you," I hate to admit it but I was probably annoyed as I walked into the bedroom. There was a reason JJ brought me coffee in bed every morning — and it was about more than just romance. "What are you saying?"

He was agitated now, upset that I wasn't getting his point, "Frunk tomato for thing house!"

A jolt went through me then, every nerve ending

tingled. Doctors sometimes call it word salad, a jumble of unrelated words tumbling about — they may as well be chunks of tomato and carrot for all the sense they make to the listener. To the speaker, it's a desperate struggle to be understood, and JJ was upset, growing more and more distressed. He was fighting to force his brain to capture the words he knew he needed, to explain what was happening to him. He was lying on the bed, flat on his back with his hands folded over his chest, and I could see his knuckles whitening as he gripped them, desperate to hold on to the thread that connected him to the world. I reached out to comfort him, laying my hand on his, but he jerked them away violently, and wouldn't look at me, "NO!"

He looked nauseous, so I grabbed a salad bowl for him to hold in the car — we were going to the hospital.

There it was — BOVITZ — but it was on the wrong side. It was automatic when I walked into the ICU, the reflexive glance at the whiteboard listing the patients by room number with their Attending Physician noted in the next column so the nurses knew who to call with questions and updates. I was accustomed to seeing my name up there. But not on the patient side. It was jarring.

It was midday now, and JJ was finally settled in his room. Well, *settled* may be an overstatement, but at least he was out of the ER. He lay on the bed, heavily sedated, his head covered in electrodes attached to color coded cords that transmitted his brain waves to a monitor, which was in turn being watched closely for signs of non-convulsive seizure activity. A bag of saline dripped through the IV in his right arm, while a catheter drained his urine into a clear bag hooked to the side of the bed, and another monitor displayed his vital signs from its position on the wall. He moaned and shifted slightly, as the blood pressure cuff inflated, but he would be out through the night after the amount of medication he'd received to stop the seizures.

He had been in status epilepticus, at risk of lasting damage to his brain from persistent seizure activity, and assessment had been complicated by the fact that once he was unconscious, there were no physical signs to go by. This was because of where the seizure focus was — in his temporal lobe, an area involved in both language and emotional processing, but the aberrant signals did not extend to his limbs and his body did not convulse.

Rather, the short-circuit in his brain trapped him in the darkest corner of his mind, held him captive in a place of sheer terror and abject misery, stripped the world of all its beauty and left him in the darkness. It stole his words too, left him utterly alone. Later, he explained that this was why he had pulled his hands away from me so violently when I'd tried to comfort him: he had been consumed with feelings of such hopelessness and despair, in such a desolate and unforgiving place, that he couldn't bear to look at my face or feel my touch, for fear that his mind might attach a whisper of that darkness to me.

Meg, with her knack for knowing what you need before you do, arrived bearing lunch and trash mags. When her smiling face appeared in the doorway, and suddenly I could exhale, I was suffused with gratitude. I couldn't tell her that though, because I promptly fell into her arms, sobbing and incoherent. I'm not sure how long I wept, or how long Meg sat quietly beside me and held my hand. But when eventually I could breath again, we decided that if there had ever been day for an afternoon cocktail, this was it.

We found ourselves at the dive bar just up the street,

and as we waited for our drinks I said, "Thank you Meg... I'm sorry I lost it like that."

She turned to face me, "Did I ever tell you what happened to our new windows?" she asked. When I shook my head, she told me how a few days after she and Brian had all their windows replaced, they noticed that several of the frames were bent. So they called the company, and a guy was sent over to take a look. When he saw what they were talking about, he laughed, and explained that's exactly what the frames are designed to do — when the pressure builds up between the panes, the frame pops open to vent it, to prevent the glass from breaking.

"Sometimes, you just need to pop a vent," Meg said, taking a sip of her Sauvignon Blanc.

JJ came home with some new medications and carried on with the chemotherapy. He was responding beautifully, and most people outside of our immediate circle didn't even know he had a brain tumor — he wanted it that way. He dreaded being known as *JJ, the Poor Guy With Cancer*. He just wanted to be *JJ*. Or maybe, *JJ, Culby and Charlie's Dad*. Life was good then, almost normal for a time. Filled with playdates and soccer games and big Family Dinners with our loved ones, camping and rafting and JJ's growing obsession with fishing. He'd fallen in love with it, and took great joy in sharing the fun. And he was good luck too — without fail, whoever he brought out caught something. Although JJ, himself, never caught a single fish.

∾

When Yucky started growing again, about a year later, proton therapy was the recommended treatment. It was relatively new, and there were only six centers in the country where it was offered; luckily for us, one was in Seattle. So JJ stayed with my friend Meredith and her family for six weeks, sleeping in their guest room and riding his bike in for daily treatments. There, his head would be secured in a mask that had been molded to fit his face exactly, and bolted to a table to guard against any inadvertent movement. Meanwhile, a huge particle accelerator known as a synchrotron was spinning protons at speeds fast enough to destroy cancer cells with their energy, and those protons were then aimed with surgical precision at the tumor, where they released their fatal load. It was amazing. It was successful. It gave us eighteen months of memories.

~

Dr. M called in the spring of 2016 to discuss the latest MRI results, and we could hear in his voice that it wasn't good news. The tumor was growing again, and this time our options were few. JJ's only shot at survival now was a clinical trial. There was one ongoing at City of Hope in southern California that he would likely qualify for, but it was a trial and there were no guarantees, despite some positive early data. And it would mean living there for the duration. A complicated proposition. We sat on the edge of our bed, the phone lying between us, Dr. M's gentle voice coming through the speaker. The other option, he explained, was a medication that had been shown to delay the onset of debilitating symptoms, but did not affect lifespan.

Lifespan. As in, the entirety of one's life.

The implication sucked all the air from my lungs, made my heart shiver. But only for a moment, then I reflexively turned my mind's eye away — I would not allow it to linger on the shadows. To acknowledge them was to give them form, and thus, power. I will admit, they did crowd in sometimes against my will, during a quiet soak in the tub for example, and every once in a while a tendril would catch me off guard. Slip past my defenses and blindside me with a vision of... *after.* But if I looked straight at it, I might start to crumble. And once I began to crumble, I might just disintegrate completely, and I couldn't risk that — what if I wasn't strong enough to pull it back together? The only safe thing was to avert my gaze.

I had become a skilled compartmentalizer. When I put on my white coat and morphed into Dr. B, I had learned to seal off my own story so as to focus on my patients fully, and without distraction. Just as I expected JJ's doctors to do. And at the end of the day, when I hung up my stethoscope, I stepped back into myself, into my family, into our life. There, I guarded the flame of hope flickering in my belly with the ferocity of an ancient firekeeper, whose success or failure would determine the fate of their clan. I focused solely on the light, steadfastly ignoring the darkness creeping in around the edges. JJ's mantra had become our soundtrack over the years, "We don't know what's gonna happen tomorrow, but we know we have today, so let's not waste it!"

"So," JJ said, "either I just accept that I'm going to die... or I take a chance on something that might or might not work, but even if it doesn't help me, it could help someone else down the road?"

I nodded slowly.

"I want to see my sons grow up," he said, taking my hands in his, "I want them to know I did everything I could. I'm not ready to give up, Doll."

26

THIRD FALL

The first time I walked beside grief, I didn't recognize it.

"I don't think I love you enough, and I don't think I ever will," my boyfriend had said flatly, from behind the steering wheel of the 1970 Volkswagen Westfalia that had been our home-base for the last nine months. We were in our 20's, young and exuberant and seeking adventure, and after spending months on the road exploring Mexico and Central America, we had returned to San Diego with a plan to drive across the country to New York where we would work for the summer and save up for our next expedition — we were negotiating the details, I had fallen in love with Guatemala and wanted to return, he thought we should go someplace new.

"What?" I was sure I had misunderstood him. I mean, we were happy, and in love, and planning our next adventure — weren't we?

"I don't think you should come to New York with me," he said, staring straight ahead through the dirty windshield, still coated with the dust of the Sonoran Desert.

I was dumbstruck. Stupefied. Pixilated. I did *not* see this coming — had we been having two different relationships all this time? I mean, we'd just driven from Southern California to Central America and back, spent every moment together. We'd scaled ancient ruins tucked deep into the Guatemalan jungle, learned to scuba dive in the Bahia Islands, slept in hammocks under the stars on deserted stretches of the Mexican shore. We'd been stranded on an uninhabited cay in the Gulf of Honduras, and had to swim to the nearest island for rescue. We'd survived engine breakdowns and culinary misadventures and the theft of almost all of our underwear. We had embraced it, and each other. This was completely out of the blue. Or at least, that's what I thought.

And apparently, my fight or flight response kicked in immediately, because without another word I flung the door open, leapt out of the car, and sprinted full-speed down the street. It didn't matter that I was wearing flip flops and no bra, I ran until I couldn't run any more.

He dropped me off in Memphis, Tennessee on a warm, rainy day. I wore a long flowy dress (because it was comfortable) and a big straw hat (because it didn't fit in my bag) which I clutched to my head in the gusty wind as he drove away. It would be six hours before the train left for Chicago, and I had no idea what to do with myself. I must have been quite a pathetic sight, standing there in the rain, weeping and forlorn as the car faded into the horizon, the gauzy fabric of my dress plastered to my wet skin like a catsuit, struggling to keep control of that ridiculous hat, suitcases in a puddle on the sidewalk beside me. It was so maudlin, I could practically hear the score of a low budget melodrama in the background.

"Hey there, darlin'!" a middle aged man wearing an

apron and bow tie called to me as he emerged from the restaurant across the street. "You look like you need to come in outta this rain, girl!" He jogged over to me, handed me his umbrella, and picked up my soggy bags, "C'mon with me now, let's get you dried off."

He led me back across the street and into BB King's Blues Club, quiet in the mid-afternoon, save for a few tourists lingering over their lunch of barbecued ribs and pulled pork. His name was Clyde, he told me as he sat me down at the bar and handed me a towel. He'd wondered what was happening when he saw me get out of the car with my bags, and got worried when it became clear that I had nowhere to go, "I couldn't let you just stand out there soaking up the rain," he said kindly.

Sometimes it's easier to bare your soul to a stranger. To reveal your deepest fears and desires to someone with no attachment to the story, no investment in its outcome, no agenda of their own. And sometimes, if you're lucky, that stranger will appear just when you need them. I sat at the bar, sipping the hot toddy Clyde handed me, and by the time I was dry, he was well familiar with all the details of my broken heart.

"So, you're telling me," Clyde said slowly as he polished the already gleaming bartop, "you want to go back to Guatemala, but this guy wants to go someplace else?"

"Well, yes, but we're broken up now so it doesn't matter anyway," I sniffed.

"That's right," he leaned across the bar and looked me in the eye as he said matter-of-factly, "so now, what's to stop you from following your heart?"

Hmmm... I thought, sipping my hot toddy.

It was too late when the boyfriend called a few weeks later, tearful and apologetic and filled with regret. I had

already made up my mind: I was going back to Guatemala.
And I was going alone.

The thing is, I just didn't *get* it.

His mother had died, you see, not long after we started
dating. At the time, I thought he had handled it well. He
had nursed her through a long illness, and I naively
assumed that had somehow prepared him for her death. I
believed him when he said he was fine. After all, I had never
suffered a loss that profound, thus my abject failure to
recognize the enormity of it — it reached beyond the
perimeter of my imagination. I didn't understand then, that
it had been a loss so devastating he couldn't even look at it —
that he'd had to lock it away, seal it off completely, or risk
being consumed by it. I hadn't learned yet, how cunning
grief is, how devious. I didn't appreciate its tendency to hide
in the darkness, festering and shape shifting as long as it is
ignored, until inevitably, it finds a crack to slip through.
That when it does finally appear it is often unrecognizable,
misdirected, and prone to irrational acts.

I wish I had.

I wish I'd been kinder, more generous, more forgiving.

I wish I'd known then, how to offer him grace.

But I didn't. Wouldn't, for a very long time. I was young
and free, as Clyde had pointed out. My whole life stretched
out in front of me, vast and filled with unimagined emprise,
mortality's horizon obscured by the twists and turns of an
uncarved path just waiting to be explored — I had all the
time in the world. And I knew in my bones that the key to
my next chapter lay in the heart of that tiny war-torn
country, a four hour flight from Chicago, and a world away.
It didn't occur to me to look beyond that.

But now, three decades and several iterations later, time was suddenly finite. And precious. Every choice would require the sacrifice of another now, it was basic math.

~

One day that third fall, I woke up feeling like my skin didn't fit. Like its shape had somehow morphed while I was sleeping, strange new nooks and unfamiliar crannies everywhere I probed. My whole landscape had shifted. Long valleys stretched out where hills once rolled, mountains rose from the ocean floor, great canyons cracked into existence. Old growth forests faded into desert, patches of new growth leafed out in unexpected places. I rolled onto my back, and as my breasts fell toward my armpits, I realized for the first time and with a startling clarity: *I am 52 years old.*

Not that I minded being 52 per se, it's just that the number threw me. Suddenly, I could see the horizon.

~

A short while later, I was sitting on my bed immersed in biostatistics calculations, when I heard Culby say from the kitchen,

"C'mon Charlie, why won't you make me some eggs?"

"Because I'm tired of always making you food," Charlie replied. "Make your own eggs."

"How bout some waffles then?"

"Culby," Charlie said, "you can do some stuff for yourself. I'm not the *mom*."

I looked up at that. Felt that same stabbing pain in the center of my chest.

"They're still little, Doll," I heard JJ whisper again. "They need you now, more than ever."

He was right. Culby was in eighth grade at the Tiny School now, and Charlie had started sixth grade at the Arts School. They were in transition — morphing from Little Kids into Teenagers at the speed of light, trying on various attitudes and opinions and hairstyles, testing the limits of their new powers, unfolding their wings. I had long been banned from helping with math homework, as I only ever made it worse, but when Culby said, "Mom, I don't like your help with homework, but I like your help with life-stuff," I took it as a win.

Life-stuff. They no longer required a chaperone for school field trips or help tying their shoes — now they needed advice about personal hygiene and early morning erections. Their questions were growing with them, as their worlds expanded beyond our fortress, as they navigated the path toward manhood. And frankly, there are some things along the way that you just don't want to talk to your mother about — they needed their dad. And they grieved him anew at each developmental stage, because there were always new things to miss, things I struggled to anticipate, having never been an adolescent boy myself. Nevertheless, I had to figure it out.

They need more of me.

I closed my laptop, and joined them in the kitchen.

"You're right Char, you're not the mom," I said, pulling them in close for a hug. "Who wants pancakes?"

That afternoon, I cut my class load in half. And when I told the boys that I was going to slow down my pace with school so that I could have more time with them, they were elated, "Thanks, Mom!" they shouted, throwing themselves into my arms. And we got to work tightening up the wheels of our tricycle.

~

I took a bag of peas out of the freezer. It had been opened previously, so the white plastic was now rolled over on itself and held closed by a purple rubber band stretched twice around its girth. I pulled the band off and set it on the countertop, measuring a cup of peas and putting them in the small colander to thaw. And as I was rolling the bag closed again, I noticed that purple rubber band, lying there. How its shape was distorted. Definitely smaller than when it had been pulled taut to contain the peas, but clearly not back to its original form, with uneven edges and an occasional out-pouching making it more of a free-form shape than a circle now. It had been stretched to capacity and then frozen solid there, its outline permanently altered. Sure, as it warmed up, it became softer, more flexible, approaching something resembling its original shape as it was pulled toward its equilibrium. But having been tested in the extreme, its very molecules had changed. It sprang back, yes, but it was a different shape now.

Like its skin didn't fit.

~

On September 24, 2019, Nancy Pelosi, Speaker of the House of Representatives, announced a formal impeachment inquiry into our 45th president, stemming from his "perfect" phone call with Ukrainian President Volodymyr Zelensky.

I'm embarrassed to admit it, but it was only then that I

actually woke up to the truth that lies beyond the caricature of the cartoon villain. Saw the very real danger that he posed, recognized his appetite for authoritarianism, his desire to sow chaos and discord and to profit from it. Only then did I understand that once he had tasted real power, he would stop at nothing to tighten his grip on it, and that this buffoon, painted orange and stuffed full of bombast, was also an experienced con-man with not one strand of moral fiber to stand in the way of his pursuit. And he was no longer surrounded by any of those professional people I had envisioned making the actual decisions. Having "purged the swamp" of all but its monsters, his court now consisted solely of quivering sycophants clinging desperately to his coattails, rabid in their desire to wield power, and voracious in their quest for it.

Yet the truth of it is, he didn't create the deep divisions in our society — he just revealed them, deepened them, weaponized them. Those fissures in our country's soul are ours to heal, the torn fabric of our communities, ours to knit back together. He only had the power we granted him. I was paralyzed for a moment, imagining the world my children would inherit should he win a second term. It felt ominous, and pervasive. Existential. But that fraught thought shook me awake, forced my attention to expand, spurred me on to action. I wasn't powerless. Our democracy still stood. I had a voice.

27

THE PARACHUTE

(2016)

Hope is a bit like a spider's silk — a most delicate gossamer, strong enough to stop a bullet. Spiders, those clever creatures, are ingenious architects. They design their webs with great foresight, such that if a single strand snaps, the structure as a whole does not collapse but rather is rendered even stronger. And when that web has finally served its purpose and it is time to move on, the spider does not simply abandon it. No. The spider will consume the silk it created, absorb the nutrients there, use all that came before to fashion something new. Sometimes it will climb, then, to the greatest possible height, and strike a pose on its tiptoes with its abdomen aimed high. It will shoot long wisps of recycled silk from its spinnerets toward the sky, sculpting a parachute that will catch the wind, lifting the spider up to ride the whims of the current. To be carried near or far or someplace in-between. It is a leap of faith.

~

Our gossamer parachute deposited us at the City of Hope, in August of 2016. We landed in a small white cottage at the end of a path that wound past several other small white cottages, each surrounded by a tidy patch of green grass, and shaded by a tree or two, ringed with marigolds. It was called Hope Village. It sat at the edge of the 100 acre campus, providing shelter and a sense of community for those who lived too far away to travel to Southern California for care.

As the two of us approached #14 for the very first time — this place that would be JJ's home for the coming months, this place where our miracle would happen — a spot of blue, peeking out from the warm brown bark at the edge of the path caught my eye. I leaned closer, peering at the small hand painted rock, and read the message painted in canary yellow letters against the azure background: *HOPE*. An offering, and an edict.

The cottage was cozy. It had one room, and the door opened onto a small kitchenette with a round linoleum table for two just under the front window. Against the far wall, a set of twin beds with simple oak headboards was separated by a nightstand holding an oversized table lamp, its equally oversized shade perched at an impossible angle. A matching dresser stood directly opposite, and a mirror misted with time around the edges, hung above. The thin quilted bedspreads bore a nondescript pattern in shades of blue and gold, and there were plenty of extra blankets. It felt like a slightly worn but clean and well-cared for motel room, like you might find in any small town anywhere, and it took a minute to register the subtle reminders that we were not, in fact, on a road trip.

The thick plastic covering on the mattresses and pillows, for example, that were designed to repel body fluids and to be quickly and thoroughly sanitized. Later, we would buy a couple of cheap pillows at the nearby Target, because the squeaky crinkly noise the plastic made every time you turned your head was enough to wake you from even the deepest slumber. There were grab bars in the bathroom, and a foldable shower seat leaning in the corner too, for when standing upright was just too much. There was a large bulletin board and a supply of pushpins hanging by the front door, next to a dry erase calendar along with a pen and eraser, to help patients keep track of all their appointments and tests and treatments. The emergency call button had a long white cord that was always within reach. And there was a telephone, with all of the relevant numbers already programmed on speed dial, a handy stack of notepads and pens emblazoned with the City of Hope logo nearby.

"Honey, I'm home!" JJ announced, dropping his bag on one of the beds. "Let's go for a walk and check this place out!" he said with a grin.

So we wandered hand-in-hand through the sculpture garden and over to the rose garden, which was pretty even after the blooms faded, soft petals carpeting the pathways. We visited the Japanese garden, too, with its arced bridges crossing over a slow moving stream filled with dancing koi, and a tiny pagoda, perfect for silent reflection. We perused the dreams written on small slips of paper that covered the cherry trees in the Wishing Garden, potential miracles, every one. And we hung our wishes there among the others, bright strips of paper rustling in the wind, prayers sent off to the heavens. We spotted other painted stones here and there, tucked under a small green bush or standing out among a naked pile of grey pebbles. Always bright and cheerful, often with a message: *LOVE* or *PEACE* or *JOY*.

And we wondered who it was that left them, these small gifts of kindness. These reminders that we were not alone.

We went out for a nice dinner that night — just in case.

The next morning, we left the gentleness of peaceful gardens and dancing fish and hidden gems, and made our way to the other side. To the sharp edged land of white coats and operating rooms and MRI machines. Infusion centers and wheelchairs and emesis basins. Harsh lighting and frigid air and cafeteria coffee. Our battlefield.

The goal of the clinical trial was to harness JJ's own immune system, calling up his soldiers to defend their homeland. But they needed specialized training first, to be shaped into Navy Seals laser focused on their target. Collateral damage was of great concern, because this war was fought on sacred ground, any errant strike likely to cause irreparable harm. So the first step was to extract those soldier-cells, isolate them, and verse them in the nefarious ways of the enemy. Then they were sent into combat, via a tiny tube that had been inserted directly into JJ's brain, and was accessed by what we call a port, which kept the rest of the world from slipping inside. His soldiers fought valiantly, and at first he did remarkably well. Further evidence of his magic.

We fell into a rhythm of sorts, because human beings are nothing if not adaptable, and anything will become normalized over time, won't it? I oscillated between Hope Village and our Portland Village, utterly reliant on, and profoundly grateful for, our team of family and friends who were always where I wasn't. I would bring the boys down when they had a long weekend, but they weren't allowed to stay in the little white cottage, so we would go to a theme park, or a random hotel to play in the pool. For them, those weekends were fun little adventures, they had no idea how hard their dad was working. How valiantly he was fighting for them.

JJ came home for Thanksgiving that November. He was responding remarkably well to the treatment, and we didn't know then that it was the last Family Dinner he would host. I have a picture in my mind, one of those moments that your subconscious somehow recognizes as vital, and so files away in excruciating detail. He is standing at the head of the table holding a carving knife, the turkey he has brined and seasoned and smoked to perfection resting before him. It is dark outside, cold and rainy, but we are cozy in here, surrounded by loved ones, cushioned by holiday rituals. He is wearing one of his favorite button down shirts, the one with multicolored checks that he'd gotten at that open-air market in Italy, and his eyes twinkle as he sets down the carving knife and raises his glass in a toast.

"Happy Thanksgiving, everyone," he says, "I just want to say, how thankful I am. For you, Doll, and for Culby and for Charlie. For all of you, and for our family and friends who aren't here today but who are always with us in spirit," he swallows hard, looking down for a moment, then he looks up with a smile and says, "I just want to say, I am thankful for this life. For *all* of it."

We raised our glasses, and drank a toast to this life. To all of it.

～

Hope is a lifeline, yes. It is also a thief.

In retrospect, it is easy to recognize that those last months spent on the frontline fighting for his life were precious moments stolen from our children, from our loved ones, from us. JJ would say that he was grateful for the time he had with close friends and family when they rotated through Hope Village. That it was a blessing, those nuggets of intimacy shared with people that he cherished. He would say that of course he couldn't give up, that his children needed to know he did everything in his power to stay here with them. That he needed me to know that too.

I suspect he knew how it would end long before I did. That he accepted it long before I would. I could see it in his eyes, when he watched our sons playing chess or having a nerf-gun battle. Or when I caught him watching me prepare his favorite meal. I would stop what I was doing then, sit beside him on the hospital bed, hold his hand. And he would sweep away my tears with his thumb, "It's okay," his eyes would say, "Don't worry. You can do this."

❦

Later, his brother Bryan (yes, another Brian — we call him Y-Bri to avoid confusion) would tell me about a conversation they'd had while fishing, just before JJ started the clinical trial.

During a quiet moment, JJ had said, "Bryan, You know I've exhausted all the approved medical treatments, and I'm on to the experimental stuff now, right?"

"Yeah, but you're going to be fine," Bryan said. "We've been through this before. You're starting new and promising —"

"Yes, that's true," JJ cut him off. "But I'm not doing this for me. It's very important that you understand that. These treatments are not going to save me, that's not why I'm doing it. I'm doing it so they can learn how to save other people in the future."

Bryan resisted, not prepared to accept what he, too, knew to be true, "I'm not burying you until you're dead," he said.

"Let's not argue about whether I'll live or die," JJ said, "these treatments might extend my life for a while, but they are not cures. I need you to understand that, because I need to ask you something."

"Okay," Bryan nodded.

"I need people to understand that I see my life as a gift. Nothing is being taken away from me, or from anyone else. This extra time I've been given since I first got this tumor is a gift from God. I don't want people to see me leaving, as me being taken away from them. I want them to understand — to see that all the experiences we've had, that I've had with everyone, they are all gifts. Without this extra time, Sara and I would not have had the gifts of Culby and Charlie. I am so grateful to God for them, and for the time I've had with Sara. I'm not upset, and I want other people to see it the way that I see it — as a *gift*. Will you deliver that message for me, Bryan?"

∼

So often I feel that people who die young are exceptional. That they leave us when their work here is done. That when their blue stone with the canary yellow letters disappears beneath the water, the ripples left behind are their gifts to us. And it's up to us then, to choose what to make of them.

28

THREE YEARS

"I told them you were her sister, so they'd let you come see her," my friend Matt said as he led me through the ED waiting room toward the treatment area where his wife Laura was being evaluated for an irregular heart rhythm. I stuck the Visitor patch on my chest, following him through the heavy double doors, and as we emerged on the other side, I found I had stepped through Alice's looking glass and right into my former life. Monitors beeped, alarms sounded, the low buzz of information being exchanged a constant underneath it all. My senses were instantly on high-alert, and the doctor in me lifted her head, reflexively scanning the area. Noting the crash cart sitting outside of room 10, the nurse rushing into room 6 where the monitor showed a slowing heart rate, the aid helping a patient to the bathroom. The doctor entering orders on a computer, the nurse preparing a sterile tray for a lumbar puncture. I felt my heart rate quicken and my fingertips tingle as a wave of adrenaline surged through me. It was eerie, the feeling that came over me, both deeply familiar, and shockingly foreign. So inextricably intertwined with, well, all of it.

I'd spent years straddling a hospital bed, with one foot on the doctor side, and one foot on the patient side. Each informed the other, in ways both helpful and excruciating. Often, JJ and I would leave a doctor's appointment with two diametrically opposed interpretations of what had transpired. "Well, that's pretty good news!" he would say, with a spring in his step as we walked to the car. And I would just smile and squeeze his hand. Because I was proficient in Doctorspeak, I knew what lay in the quiet spaces. But I couldn't tell him that for an oncologist, *success* is frequently measured in weeks and months, not years and decades. Sometimes it felt like I was keeping a secret from him, walling it off so that it couldn't reach him. So that it couldn't leech his hope.

In the very beginning, JJ said to me, "Doll, I don't need you to be my doctor, I need you to be my wife." I tried my best to honor that for the rest of his life. My job was to find him the very best team, and then let them do their jobs. And also to shut up during appointments, because otherwise the doctor would end up talking to me rather than to JJ, and that drove him nuts. I was grateful every day that I was in a position to access those experts — grateful to JJ most of all, frankly, because I can't imagine how I would have gotten through medical school and residency and then all those years of working odd hours for long stretches without him there doing literally everything else. He was enmeshed in my experience of medicine, its very scaffolding. It was a precarious structure without his support.

I felt the ghost of a stethoscope around my neck, the phantom weight of a white coat on my shoulders, as I stood there in my old life. In my *before*. And in that moment, a deceptively simple truth revealed itself to me.

This isn't who I am anymore. In my after.

~

On December 18, 2019, the United States House of Representatives adopted two articles of impeachment against the 45th president of the United States, one for abuse of power and the other for obstruction of justice.

I started writing letters for Vote Forward.

~

It was a very precise moment, when the utter folly of my grand plan crystalized: I was having a bath, lying perfectly still, when the piles of bubbles floating on the scalding water suddenly and spontaneously parted, opening up a channel, a path. Clearing the way, it seemed, and revealing me to myself below. Naked.

What was I thinking? Had I really convinced myself that two young boys could have any concept of what it would mean to be uprooted from their lives, and live half the year in a foreign country? Was I actually taking their enthusiasm to mean they were capable of making a choice like that? Of course they loved the romance of the idea, the adventure of it, but obviously the reality would be another thing altogether.

The fantasy in my head had gone like this: We would be of service, my two boys and I, in Guatemala, the land of their birth, in the name of their father. They would grow up with an expansive world view, their perspectives and priorities shaped by exposure to the breadth of the human experience, their character built on compassion, their ethic on hard work, and they would go forth and do great things, leaving the world better off for them having been in it. Just like their father.

No pressure. I felt my face flush at the unmitigated grandiosity of it.

And it occurred to me, as I lay there in the cooling water, the bubbles slowly melting away, that perhaps I was in my own version of a rebound-relationship — let's call it a rebound-career choice. It was grounded in grief and fueled by magical thinking, by a deep need to honor JJ, to create something good and beautiful from the dust. I had reflexively sprung back toward the person I was before him, when the tether broke, toward the person I was the last time I was without him. But I was just like that purple rubber band — my very molecules had changed.

What I hadn't been able to see from so deep inside, was that we already *were* creating something good and beautiful from the dust. We may have started out as a wobbly tricycle, but we were finding our balance. And that's all that had mattered to JJ, all he wanted was for us to heal, and then to thrive.

And to thrive, our sons needed a solid launching pad. We were just starting to find ourselves after all, to create our new rhythm. This was not the time to upend them. Obviously.

~

It was like a fountain. Powerful and voluminous. The words flinging themselves onto the page, messy and convoluted, not consciously formed but appearing there nonetheless. Something from nothing. The release was intense, afterwards I felt uncoiled. Lighter, somehow. It was amazing.

I started writing every day. Feeling my way through the chaos. Now and then, an errant drop would separate itself from the stream, plop down right in front of me and demand my attention. Sometimes, I had to step away from it, for fear that if I peered too closely I would be sucked in, become enveloped, encased, entombed. That once inside I might lose sight of the exit, end up imprisoned there. But there were other times too. Times when I could slip in and look around. When I discovered that I could hold my grief for a moment, without being crushed. When I could recognize the beauty and the joy and the grace that live there. When I could feel gratitude, untainted by bitterness.

And on one of those days I looked up, feeling spent and at peace, and heard — nothing. There was no low hum of voices in the background. No radio or television filling the empty spaces. No white noise keeping the dark noise in my head at bay. Just, silence. I was alone with my thoughts.

And for the first time in years, that was okay.

~

The holidays were a bit more gentle that year, the memories less barbed.

For the first time, we had a living Christmas tree, in a pot. It felt like having a guest with us for a few weeks. We named him Fred, and I missed him when he went off to be happily planted among his brethren in a local watershed. Fred was too young to support the steel angel made by Haitian artisans, his limbs too thin for the old-fashioned ceramic bulbs we typically used. So we decorated him with fairy lights, and topped him with a big red bow. It brought me such joy, that little tree, it felt life-affirming somehow. Like we were a link in the chain, rather than the bolt cutter. And it assuaged my guilt on January 2nd — I had always felt like a traitor, just kicking a Christmas tree to the curb after its purpose was served.

Charlie confessed that he had known I was Santa for a while, but hadn't said anything because, "I didn't want to break the magic." Now that he was in on the secret though, he offered to take responsibility for moving the Elf on the Shelf every night, a job I happily relinquished — although I will say, not without several severe pangs of nostalgia. The very first thing Culby and I did every morning that December was hunt for the Elf, and Charlie delighted in finding ever more obscure hiding spots to keep us guessing — there were a few times that we never did find it. But Charlie would just giggle, and then wait until we were fast asleep to make the magic happen.

JJ supervised it all, from his place on the mantle, the pom pom on the end of his holiday hat dangling cheerfully, as we sifted through remembrances. And began creating new ones.

The three of us spent that New Years Eve at home together, it just felt right somehow. We made a bunch of fancy appetizers, and ate them curled up in front of the fire watching movies and playing boardgames until it was time for the countdown, the end of 2019. The start of a new decade. It felt momentous, and hopeful. I could see the sky beginning to lighten beyond the mountaintop that loomed before us, could even feel the warmth of the sun's longest rays as they stretched beyond the peak, lighting our path to the summit. I wasn't sure what lay on the other side, but I was actually starting to believe that we would make it there.

≈

This was it. The Third Anniversary.

I laughed out loud when I rolled over and saw that it was exactly 3:00.

I guess your body really does remember, I thought, as I watched the minutes tick by, the slideshow in my mind matching the numbers on the clock.

I felt myself sinking into the familiar cloak of grief then, wrapping it around me, allowing myself to be absorbed by it. Comforted by it.

"You can't lose what's real, Doll," I heard JJ whisper.

The boys stayed home from school again, and we had a pajama day, lounging in front of the fire, but instead of eating only junk food, I made chicken & dumplings and carrot cake, JJ's favorites. While I was straining the broth and shredding the chicken, Charlie came into the kitchen and with a great flourish poured himself a glass of water.

"Mom, watch!" he said with a giggle, taking a gulp, "I'm drinking dinosaur pee!" We both burst out laughing, and Culby came into the kitchen, wondering what was so funny. "Culby — every drop of water on Earth has been peed out by a dinosaur," Charlie explained gleefully. "So every time you drink water, you're drinking dinosaur pee!"

"No way," Culby said skeptically. "Mom, is that true?"

"It is, actually," I said, and we talked about how crazy it is that everything in the universe is made up of the same stuff, just in different combinations and organized in different ways. About how everything is interconnected. How we all come from the same stardust.

A vivid memory sprang to the front of my mind, unbidden. It was sometime during the snowy days just after JJ died, and I was standing in Culby's room staring absently

out the window, my mind a sped up video flashing through
images of the past and imaginings of the future, when a car
pulled up. It stopped in front of our house, and someone
jumped out with a shovel. They were all bundled up so I
couldn't tell who it was, but they quickly shoveled our
sidewalk and then jumped back in the car and drove away.

That small kindness brought me to my knees. I sank to
the floor, and wept. Tears of pain and loneliness and fear,
yes, but also of gratitude. I knew that I was completely,
absolutely, unequivocally, unqualified for the task at hand.
That I had no idea what to do, much less how to do it. But
deep in my soul, I also knew that I was not alone, no matter
how lonely I might be.

It spoke to me of the power of community. Of how we
stretch each other, teach each other, shape each other in
ways big and small. Of how we are stronger together, more
flexible, more resilient. We are social creatures after all —
we need each other in order to understand ourselves. In
order to create ourselves, even. Because while we can *think*
whatever we want about who we are (*I'm brave, I'm kind,
I'm generous...*), the fact is, it's only when circumstance
presents us with the opportunity to make a choice and then
act on it, that we actually *become* who we are.

~

"Mom," Culby said as we snuggled on the sofa after dinner
that night, "I think next year on the Anniversary, we'll just
go to school, like a normal day."

"Yeah," said Charlie, "I think we're ready."

"That would make Daddy so happy," I said, squeezing
them tight.

Culby stretched out his legs, leaning back and laying his

head on my lap, "Mom," he said, "when I turn 18, I want us to all get matching tattoos." He looked up at me from the corner of his eye, waiting to gauge my reaction.

"I'll get a tattoo with you," I grinned at him, "that's literally the only thing that would make me get one! What would you want it to be?"

He smiled softly and said, "A tricycle... obviously."

ACKNOWLEDGMENTS

Dearest Loved Ones,

I would not have made it to the other side without you.

Through my darkest hour, you graciously and lovingly gave
me the time and space that I needed to heal, without strings
or guilt or pressure. You loved me through my very worst
days, even when I was my very worst self. You listened
when I needed an ear, and talked when I needed a
distraction. You forgave me missed calls, unanswered texts,
and late responses. You understood when grief disrupted an
evening's plans, and included me even when it was
awkward to have that lone extra chair at the end of the
table.

You gifted me the knowledge that when I stumbled into
my grief hole, you would not forget me. I knew you would
be there when I found my way back out, and that you
would help me to stand up, dust myself off, and turn back
toward the future. I knew this to be true, because you did it.
Repeatedly. You comforted me with shared history and
stories and memories, because you *know* all that we lost —
after all, you lost him too.

And later, when the time came to share our story, and I
found myself overwhelmed by all of the things that come
after the actual writing of it, there you were. Offering your
singular talents and your unflinching support. Exceedingly

generous with your time, and ridiculously patient with my ignorance. I am deeply grateful.

I am especially appreciative of Kelly's artistry — your stunning cover design touches the very heart of it all... of Meg's insights, perspective, and counsel — you always have the right words... of Laura's brilliant flair — you created the perfect logo for Pepem Press, and will be part of us forever... and of Jen's passion and infinite skill-set — you are so very generous with both.

The living of this story, and the telling of it, has been a group project. Beginning to end.

So, I want to say *thank you* to my beloved family, of origin and of choice. Thank you for walking with us. Thank you for remembering JJ, and for helping our sons to remember their dad. Thank you for honoring him and his life by living as he did — filled with love and light, compassion and generosity, friendship and joy. Thank you for teaching your children about kindness and community, empathy and patience, honor and selflessness — they give me hope, and would make JJ proud.

Thank you, for shining your light into the dark spaces, and revealing all the treasures hidden there.

Thank you, for making magic.

And a special thank you to Lizzie Simon — this book would not exist without you. It was a brutal journey, soul-rending and joyous in turn. There were a thousand moments when I would have given up, were it not for your tenacious cheerleading. Thank you for your guidance, your patience, and your ruthless edits. And most of all, thank you for getting my butt in the chair.

ABOUT THE AUTHOR

Sara Harkness Bovitz came to writing after turns as a starving actress, a photojournalist, a development worker in Central America, and a medical doctor in the Pacific Northwest. Along the way she became a wife, a mother, a widow, and an only-parent. She lives with her family in Portland, Oregon, and fortunately her sense of humor remains intact. She is still a work-in-progress.

Stories matter. They have the power to forge connections, broaden perspectives, expand empathies, and soften hearts. They grant us insight, increase our tolerance, keep us flexible. Sara loves to hear stories from her readers, connect with her on instagram @sarabovitz #thetricyclebook

www.ingramcontent.com/pod-product-compliance
Lightning Source LLC
Chambersburg PA
CBHW031129090426
42738CB00008B/1027